PSALMS

THE WORSHIPFUL COACH

A BIBLE STUDY FOR COACHES WHO WANT TO WORSHIP GOD AS THEY LEAD PEOPLE

A 10-WEEK STUDY

RYAN LIMBAUGH

The Worshipful Coach: Psalms

Cross Training Publishing

www.crosstrainingpublishing.com

(308) 293-3891

ISBN: 978-1-929478-03-3

FOREWORD

In the midst of the relentless intensity of the Coaching profession, I so often find myself longing to marinate in the comforting, wonderful Psalms in God's Word!

Ryan Limbaugh's book, The Worshipful Coach, guides coaches who follow Christ on a journey through the Psalms. Limbaugh illustrates that even during the rollercoaster of fluctuating emotions in unpredictable times, God can provide for all our needs.

It is our desire at Kingdom Sports to help train coaches and athletes to compete biblically by the power of God for the glory of God. We hope this study will help you understand how to transform competition so you will glorify King Jesus in every area of your sport. You can find many other studies for coaches and athletes at www.kingdomsports.online.

Ron Brown

Director of Player Support and Outreach

University Nebraska Football

Co-founder of Kingdom Sports

www.kingdomsports.online

TABLE OF CONTENTS

WORSHIPFUL COACHES . . .

GRATITUDE

This book about worship from the Psalms would not be possible without some wonderful people who assisted me along the way. First, Tucker Winfrey spent hours formatting, editing, thinking, re-thinking, and praying with me on the details of each chapter. I am so grateful for his cheerful and valuable assistance. I also want to thank Wes Neal for his editing and application insights that he knows all too well. Second, my wife Jamie has been so supportive and helpful through the time it took to craft this book. This writing project did not press the pause button on all my other responsibilities as a husband, dad, campus missionary, church member, and so forth. Big sacrifices were made by her to relieve me of certain duties at home and elsewhere. I am so grateful for her love. Third, I want to thank all my friends and family members who are enthusiastic worshipers of God. Some of you are coaches and athletes. Others are business owners and homemakers. But no matter what you do as a profession, it is your passion to worship God with your whole heart that has influenced and empowered me to more zealously give Him praise. Thank you for your example of reverence and celebration.

INTRODUCTION

In eternity past the one triune God, who exists in three distinct persons (Father, Son, and Holy Spirit), enjoyed perfect fellowship, love, harmony, and holiness. Nothing was wrong or empty. Everything was right and beautiful. But in an act of great love and with a desire to magnify His glory, He created the universe, this world, and His crowning achievement—humanity. He created man in His own image with a desire to be in sweet fellowship with humanity forever. He even gave man dominion over the earth to subdue it.

But man wasn't content to have sweet fellowship with God. Man wanted to be God. He wanted to take hold of God's glory and make it his own. This tragedy is revealed with man's interaction with the serpent in the midst of the garden. Man made the decision to walk away from the goodness and sweetness of God in order to test the waters of self-autonomy and independence from God. When he made that decision, he thrust all of humanity and the entirety of the world under the curse of sin. Childbirth became hard. Work became hard. Marriage became hard. Life became hard. Moreover, the ultimate curse of sin was eternal death.

But God, in His great love and for His own glory, was unwilling to stand idly by and watch all of humanity perish forever. He promised redemption. He promised a Redeemer. For hundreds of years, He made promises to man, established covenants with man, cared for man, delivered man, spoke to man, and demonstrated His love for man.

Then, all of a sudden, according to the eternal plan of God, the second member of the Trinity, the eternal Son of God, broke into human history and was born of a virgin—fully God and fully human. It was a miracle beyond our comprehension. Jesus Christ (Son of God—Son of Man—Fully God—Fully Man) lived a perfect, holy, loving, compassionate life. He healed the sick. He raised the dead. He made blind people see and deaf people hear. He loved the unlovable. He touched the untouchable. He embraced the outcasts. He lived perfectly, loved powerfully, and served humbly.

He lived the life that you and I were originally supposed to live. And what did He get for it? Jealousy, envy, and hatred. Ultimately, He received torture and murder at the hands of sinners like you and me. But more than that, He was punished by God the Father as if He had lived the kind of life we have lived—lying, deceiving, lusting, bragging, cheating, hating, slandering. God the Father exercised righteous wrath on His sinless Son. Why? Because we needed redemption. We needed a Redeemer. So, "He made Him who knew no sin to be sin on our behalf, so that we might become the righteousness of God in Him!" Once the penalty for sin was paid, Jesus Christ cried out, "It is finished!" He died and was buried.

On the third day He rose from the dead, defeating death, sin, darkness, and hell itself. The victory was won, so that anyone who believes in Him will have eternal life, be in sweet fellowship with God, joyfully live for His glory, and experience His blessing. You can be rescued from the power, pollution, and penalty of sin and saved to the power of Christ's resurrection, purity of Christ's righteousness, and presence of Christ's glory forever. You can be indwelled and empowered with the same Spirit that raised Jesus from the dead. All you have to do is "confess with your mouth that Jesus is Lord and believe in your heart that God raised Him from the dead, and you will be saved" (Romans 10:9).

That is the Gospel. That is the good news of salvation. If you believe it and have been redeemed by it, right now would be a great time for you to pause and give praise to God and thanksgiving to Jesus Christ. Now would be a great time to offer worship to your Lord.

Some big questions still remain, however. What does the Gospel have to do with your life right now?

- What does that Gospel have to do with your coaching?
- What does that Gospel have to do with your marriage?
- What does that Gospel have to do with your work ethic?
- What does that Gospel have to do with your church involvement?
- What does that Gospel have to do with your social media use?

The Gospel has everything to do with all of that! It gives you spiritual power and proper perspective to live and coach effectively for the glory of God. God's will is to work His Gospel truth into the very fabric of your heart so that you will be a coach who possesses the power of God wherever you go.

I have written this study to help you be a worshipful coach in a culture full of idolatry. Worship is the celebration of being in a covenant relationship with the God of the Gospel. It is the expression of praise to the Redeemer. Your team needs to see what a worshiper is like. Your family needs to know what a worshiper is. Your colleagues need to know the difference between a coach who lives for sports and one who lives for God. At the end of the day, people everywhere need to be around genuine worshipers. So, my prayer is that God will equip and empower you to be a worshipful coach who continually gives praise to God and influences others to do the same. As you engage in this study of God's Word, may the King of kings and Lord of lords thrill your heart with the awesomeness of Himself.

For our Praiseworthy King,

Ryan Limbaugh

FORMAT

The format for this manual is pretty simple.
These are the component parts of each chapter:

CHAPTER TITLE

Summarizes the key concept in one word or phrase.

STUDY STARTER

Helps you understand the importance and relevance of the spiritual truths you're about to study.

STUDY PASSAGE

Gives you the designated biblical text to read and study for the chapter.

STUDY HELP

Provides insight into the meaning of words, interpretation of statements, and explanation of concepts.

STUDY QUESTIONS

Asks questions about the passage you must investigate and answer.

STUDY SUMMARY

Condenses the passage into one singular statement so you can understand the "big idea" of the text.

COACHING CONNECTION

Takes the Study Summary and transfers it to the world of coaching so you can clearly see the Spirit-intended applications of the Word of God on your life as a Christian coach.

KEYS TO WINNING

Guides you to meditate on the spiritual truths in the text and how they should shape your own heart and life as a coach.

GAME CHANGER

Points you to the person and work of Jesus Christ to help you be a worshipful coach through the power of the Gospel.

ONE BIG THING

Asks you to consider the most significant lesson you should take with you from the chapter.

IMPACT PRAYER

Motivates you to seek the Lord's help in applying the truths you have learned in each study.

KINGDOM COACHING

It is an approach to coaching that focuses not just on winning games but on developing the whole person - body, mind, and spirit. By helping athletes grow in their physical abilities, mental toughness, and faith, Kingdom coaches seek to honor God through the way they lead and serve others. The principles of teamwork, discipline, and perseverance that are key to success in sports can also be important values in Christian discipleship. Each chapter will apply biblical principles to the areas of coaching.

STRATEGY

The strategy for this manual is quite simple.
This is our recommendation:

Recruit a group of coaches to walk through the study with you. These coaches do not have to be Christians to join the study. As a matter of fact, we encourage you to reach out to all coaches you think would consider participating.

Secure a copy of this training manual for every coach who participates in the study. You can order more copies at www.crosstrainingpublishing.com

Appoint a leader for the weekly group study. This leader can be a coach, former coach, spiritual leader, or pastor. The key criteria are that this person is a Christian who understands coaches, pursues Christ, and is willing to put in a little extra work to make the group study a powerful time in the Word of God. The group leader has the liberty to elaborate on the text and press into areas that are not necessarily covered in each lesson. This manual is merely a guide. There is freedom to take the study deeper and wider for more growth.

Schedule a weekly meeting day and time for 10-12 weeks. Allocate 45 to 60 minutes for the group study. Put the dates and times in your calendar and consider them high priority.

Invest 30-60 minutes on your own prior to the study familiarizing yourself with the study passage, reading it, and answering the study questions. Consider the Study Summary, Coaching Connection, and Keys to Winning. Go to the group study ready to participate, ask questions, provide insight, seek help, and sharpen your fellow coaches in their pursuit of Christ.

Encourage one another throughout the week with the truths you are learning. As iron sharpens iron, so one coach will sharpen another.

Trust God to do a powerful work in your heart and life. The Word of God is living and active, sharper than a two-edged sword. It pierces to the division of soul and spirit, joints, and marrow, and discerns the thoughts and intentions of the heart. It will do heart surgery on you if you surrender yourself to it. So, give yourself to this study and watch God work powerfully in and through you in the details of your coaching and personal life.

Read the Scouting Report prior to Week One. Just as you try to know as much as you can about your opponent before you play them, you need to know as much as you can about the context of Psalms before you study it.

Don't worry if you can't find another coach to study with you. The best way to profit from this study is with a group of other coaches, but you can certainly do it on your own. If you're a Christian, you have the Spirit of Christ living in you. He will give you illumination along the way. So don't let your isolation from other like-minded coaches discourage you. We encourage you to ask your local pastor, FCA staff, or church leader to walk through it with you. Anyone who loves the Lord and wants to grow into greater maturity could be a great study partner.

SCOUTING REPORT

ON PSALMS

The TITLE of Psalms

- The book of Psalms is the collective songbook of God's people. It was originally called "The Book of Praises" in the original Hebrew language because of its emphasis on giving praise to God. When this "Book of Praises" was translated into the Greek language it was designated as the "Psalms," which basically means "the plucking of strings." The idea is that they are songs with instrumental accompaniment. They have the combination of lyrics and instruments. That's the basic idea.

- There are 150 different "psalms" or "praises." One hundred and sixteen of those have titles at the beginning. Those titles give specific information like authorship, musical instructions, historical occasion, and dedications. These titles were helpful to the worship leaders and worshipers as they prepared for corporate worship and engaged in it.

The AUTHORSHIP of Psalms

- As is the case for every book in the Bible, God is the ultimate author of the book of Psalms. Second Timothy 3:16 teaches us the principle of divine authorship, "All Scripture is breathed out by God." And 2 Peter 1:21 reiterates it, "No prophecy was ever produced by the will of man, but men spoke from God as they were carried along by the Holy Spirit."

- On the human side, there are at least seven known authors:

  ~ King David – wrote at least 73.

  ~ Sons of Korah – wrote 10 (Psalm 42; 44-49; 84, 85, 87).

  ~ Asaph – wrote 12 (Psalm 50; 73-83).

  ~ Solomon – wrote two (Psalm 72, 127).

  ~ Heman – wrote one (Psalm 88).

  ~ Ethan – wrote one (Psalm 89).

  ~ Moses – wrote one (Psalm 90).

  ~ Anonymous writers – wrote 50 of the psalms.

- The time-range of the writing of Psalms spans about 900 years (c. 1400 BC – 500 BC).

The THEME of Psalms

- The Psalms cover a wide variety of issues, from corporate worship to personal depression. They address practical matters of daily life and theological issues such as God's sovereignty. But, undoubtedly, the central theme of Psalms is worship. It is a songbook of praises to God. It is the combination of God's revelation to His people and their response of faith to Him.

The STRUCTURE of Psalms

Psalms is divided into five "books."

- Book 1: Psalm 1-41
- Book 2: Psalm 42-72
- Book 3: Psalm 73-89
- Book 4: Psalm 90-106
- Book 5: Psalm 107-150

The STUDY of Psalms:

How should we read and study Psalms today? We should do so redemptively. We should understand each psalm's historical context, grammar, and vocabulary with the intention to accurately grasp the bigger story of worship that God is communicating to us. If we prayerfully and earnestly study each of the selected psalms, God will meet us there. He will reveal Himself. He will expose our needs. And we will strengthen our praise of Him. The deeper we go in our knowledge of Him, the higher we will go in our worship of Him.

PREGAME QUESTIONS

1. When you hear the word "worship," what comes to your mind? What activities, expressions, places, or people immediately appear in your head?

2. Everyone understands why it is important to be a "disciplined" coach, a "demanding" coach, an "excellent" coach, and a "detail-oriented" coach. But why is it important to be a "worshipful" coach?

3. What are your two favorite worship songs or hymns? Explain why?

4. At the end of this study in 10-12 weeks, what would you like to see God have done in your heart and life?

5. The title of this study is ***The Worshipful Coach*** because that is God's desire for you. He wants men and women who will worship Him day-in and day-out, no matter what their circumstances are. You have an incredible opportunity to be God's worshipful coach on your campus, with your team, and in your family. Will you write out a simple prayer asking God to make you a more worshipful person through this study of Psalms?

____

____

____

____

____

____

____

____

6. If possible, choose another coach to be your partner in this study for mutual encouragement, accountability, and prayer. You can hold one another accountable to do the pre-work, thoughtfully answer the questions, and implement the keys to winning in your coaching. If you can secure a partner within the group, write his/her name down here and make a plan to communicate with him/her each week.

____

____

____

____

____

____

____

____

NOTES:

★ ★ ★

CHAPTER ONE
WORSHIPFUL COACHES
DELIGHT IN GOD'S WORD

PSALM 1

STUDY STARTER

You may be familiar with the following lyrics.

Here's a little song I wrote

You might want to sing it note for note

Don't worry, be happy

In every life we have some trouble

But when you worry you make it double

Don't worry, be happy...

The song, of course, is the universally famous "Don't Worry, Be Happy" by Bobby McFerrin. It has a pleasant tune and a positive message. The dictionary defines being happy as being delighted in something, or someone, being glad, and having pleasure. Pretty much the flow of this song.

But the question this song fails to answer is: How can I really be happy when things go wrong?

You may be thinking, *Bobby McFerrin never went 2-12 in one season with less talent returning for the second season!!!* And you're probably right.

But even though the song above doesn't answer the important question of how to be happy, Psalm 1 actually does!

In the very first psalm, we find the source of true happiness. Let's dive into the ocean of God's Word and begin to swim in the deep waters of authentic happiness.

STUDY PASSAGE

1 *[1]Blessed is the man*

who walks not in the counsel of the wicked,

nor stands in the way of sinners,

nor sits in the seat of scoffers;

2 *but his delight is in the law of the Lord,*

and on his law he meditates day and night.

3 *He is like a tree*

planted by streams of water

that yields its fruit in its season,

and its leaf does not wither.

In all that he does, he prospers.

4 *The wicked are not so,*

but are like chaff that the wind drives away.

5 *Therefore the wicked will not stand in the judgment,*

nor sinners in the congregation of the righteous;

6 *for the Lord knows the way of the righteous,*

but the way of the wicked will perish.

STUDY HELP

- ***"blessed"*** – conveys the idea of happiness. Life is good for the coach who is blessed. Do such blessed coaches face trials, tribulations, and temptations? Yes. But, in whatever circumstance they find themselves, they are happy, fortunate...and "blessed."

- ***"the law of the LORD"*** – is the merciful revelation of the will of God. It is fixed and written. Explicitly, it is His Word—the Bible.

- ***"delight"*** – carries the idea of great pleasure. The basic meaning of "delight" is to feel great favor towards something.

- ***"meditates"*** – means to ponder and give serious consideration to selected information. Meditation stresses careful, diligent attention to Scripture, like in seeking God's guidance.

- ***"chaff"*** – debris separated from the seed in threshing grain. It is worthless and easily scattered. Heavy kernels fall to the ground while the useless chaff is blown away.

- *"knows the way of the righteous"* – in this context, can mean to take care of, or provide for, with affectionate concern. "Knowing" in Hebrew understanding is not simply intellectual knowledge about something or someone. Rather, it is the end result of experience and relationship. The Lord does not merely have an intellectual knowledge about the way of the righteous, He attends to them and takes care of them.

STUDY QUESTIONS

1. We see a progression of sin in verse 1 that the blessed man avoids. Observe the key verbs. What is the natural progression of unrepentant sin?

___

___

___

___

2. What does it mean to "delight" in the law of the LORD (v. 2)? How has God's Word been a delight to you?

___

___

___

___

3. Those who delight in the law of the LORD spend time meditating on it. How might meditation on God's Word play out in how you relate to your athletes with their differing personalities?

___

___

___

___

4. The psalmist compares a meditating worshiper to what (v. 3)? How does this word-picture affect your desire to have your coaching be rooted in God's Word?

____

____

____

5. In contrast to the "blessed" man, how does the psalmist illustrate the life of the wicked (v. 4)? How does the illustration of chaff challenge you to be deeply rooted in God's Word?

____

____

____

6. What is the difference between the outcome of the life of the wicked and the life of the righteous (vv. 5-6)?

____

____

____

STUDY SUMMARY

Being rooted in God's Word brings satisfying delight, or happiness and pleasure. It guarantees God's blessings on your life. On the other hand, choosing the path of wickedness—contrary to God and His ways—will damage your life and destroy your soul for all eternity.

COACHING CONNECTION

According to Psalm 1, the worshipful coach's greatest happiness is not found in wins and championships, but in delighting in God's Word and pointing others to His goodness.

KEYS TO WINNING

▶ **VIDEO GUIDE AT KINGDOMSPORTS.ONLINE**

▶ THE REALITY OF DELIGHTING IN GOD'S WORD

The launchpad for everything the psalmist talks about in this chapter is having delight, or great pleasure, in God's Word. This is important to know because it changes our outlook on pursuing God and His ways of coaching. Having delight, or great pleasure is not something that we obtain by simply trying harder. Rather we experience it as God transforms our hearts.

Imagine you have an athlete on your team who is struggling to perform in games as well as he was earlier in the season. How would you solve that problem? Perhaps you discover that the athlete is both physically and mentally fatigued. Simple fix. You rest him/her for a short time.

But what about another athlete who doesn't give much effort because he/she has lost his/her desire? How would you solve that issue? The solution is much harder because the problem isn't performance. It's passion. It isn't a physical issue; it's a desire issue.

Lack of desire will not be corrected simply by physical work...or rest. Lack of desire will be corrected only by a change of heart. In the same way, delighting, or taking great pleasure, in God's Word isn't simply a result of grinding, but a gift of grace—God's kindness and blessing, indicating His favor.

If you're a follower of Christ, He has given you a new heart (2 Corinthians 5:17). And in this new heart, He has given you the desire to know Him more deeply. This is exactly why He has given us His Word—because it's in His Word that we discover more deeply who He is.

1. On a scale of 1-10, how consistently do you delight, or take great pleasure, in God's Word?

1 2 3 4 5 6 7 8 9 10

2. What might be pulling your heart away from delighting fully in God's Word?

____

____

____

▸ THE RESULT OF DELIGHTING IN GOD'S WORD

As you delight, or take great pleasure, in God's Word, you will see blessing and prosperity in your coaching and family life now and in eternity with Christ.

When you think about "blessing" and "prosperity" you may be tempted to think in terms of what the world says is prosperous. For example, winning several championships and multiple "Coach of the Year" awards.

But as you meditate on God's Word you find that your desires begin to conform to God's desires. What is wise from the world's perspective is now foolish to you, having God's perspective. What is a blessing from the world's perspective is now seen clearly for how shallow it is from God's perspective.

When you are immersed in God's Word, He transforms the way you interact with your spouse, children, students, athletes, assistants, and everyone around you. He transforms the way you handle circumstances. He transforms your attitudes and actions, and your happiness is more consistent.

As you pursue God's Word you will see prosperity in every aspect of your life. Again, maybe not how the world would think of prosperity, but in ways that result in more glory to God—recognizing Him for who He is,—more delight in His grace—His undeserved favor toward you,—and more love for those around you, including your family, friends, and athletes.

1. How have you seen the Lord's blessing on your life and relationships because of your desire and discipline to follow Him?

____

____

____

2. What reasons do you have to worship the Lord with your whole heart today?

____

____

____

____

GAME CHANGER

This psalm gives us a very clear contrast between the life of the righteous and the life of the wicked. As we read the psalm it can become overwhelming to think about what is required to be counted as righteous.

We simply cannot fulfill this call to righteousness. We have walked in the counsel of the wicked. We have stood in the way of sinners. We have sat in the seat of scoffers.

In fact, at certain points in our lives, we have been the wicked, the sinners, and the scoffers. Romans 3:12 quotes Psalm 14 and makes this universal declaration, "no one does good, no not one."

While none of us is righteous, there is One who is. What we see in Psalm 1 is really a description of Jesus. He didn't walk in the counsel of the wicked; He confronted their hypocritical hearts. He didn't stand in the way of sinners; He made a way for sinners to be saved. He didn't sit in the seat of scoffers; He hung on the cross enduring the punishment of those who scoffed at Him below.

Jesus lived the righteous life that we couldn't live, died the death that we deserved, and rose from the grave with victory over death, sin, and Satan. He undeservingly inherited the punishment for sin so that we could undeservingly inherit the prize of His righteousness.

Your eternity doesn't hinge on what you're able to do, but on what Jesus did on your behalf. He is "Jesus Christ the righteous" (1 John 2:1), and He graciously gives that righteousness to you.

However, more than saving you by His righteousness, He plants you by streams of water and fills you with His righteousness. As you celebrate the grace you've been given, you can commit to living your life, including coaching your athletes, rooted in the life-giving, soul-delighting words of the Lord. You now have the Spirit of Jesus to guide you into this most blessed and happy life.

ONE BIG THING

What is the most significant lesson for you from this chapter?

____

____

____

____

____

____

IMPACT PRAYER

Father in Heaven, thank You for graciously giving us your written Word so that we may know You more fully. Create in us a heart that delights in and meditates on Your Word. Thank You for sending Christ to live the righteous life that we couldn't live in order to give us the joyful life we don't deserve. Strengthen us to be trees planted by streams of water that produce abundant fruit for the glory of Christ alone. Amen.

KINGDOM COACHING

▸ THE ULTIMATE COACHING CLINIC

Most of us pay closer attention to instructions when we know that the instructions will help us experience what we want to experience. That's one reason you go to coaching clinics. Along with enjoying fellowship with other coaches.

Interestingly, that's also true in reading God's words in the Bible. It's only in the "coaching clinic" of God's words that we learn how to experience the maximum life He has for us… as we richly fellowship with Him.

As you continue in this study, think of God's words in the Bible as the ultimate coaching clinic.

NOTES:

★ ★ ★

CHAPTER TWO

WORSHIPFUL COACHES TRUST IN GOD'S KING

PSALM 2

STUDY STARTER

Joseph Stalin was one of history's most bloodthirsty tyrants. He ruled the Soviet Union for a quarter century in the early 1900s. In pushing socialism and communism, his regime was called the reign of terror because he murdered over 10 million people in his own country and enslaved millions more in slave labor camps.

A story is told about Stalin speaking in front of a large crowd about the glories of communism. He held a chicken in his arms and methodically plucked the feathers off the chicken one by one as he spoke. Finally, the chicken was featherless. Stalin bent down, released the chicken, and it hobbled off bleeding.

Then Stalin scooped up a handful of chicken feed, dropped to his knees, and held his hand out. The wounded chicken walked back to Stalin and ate out of his hand. This, Stalin illustrated, was the glory of communism.

Stalin had a general disregard for human life primarily because he had no regard for God or God's Son, Jesus Christ. Stalin's sister gave witness that just before he died, Stalin sat up in bed, and raised his fist in the air, shaking it at God. He then fell back and died.

While not as blatant as Stalin, millions of other leaders throughout the ages have ruled, reigned, and judged with no God-consciousness and no regard for Jesus Christ. That is precisely the context of Psalm 2. So, let's now take a look at this sobering psalm that will ground us in the universal reign of His Anointed King.

STUDY PASSAGE

2 1 Why do the nations rage
and the peoples plot in vain?
2 The kings of the earth set themselves,
and the rulers take counsel together,
against the Lord and against his Anointed, saying,
3 "Let us burst their bonds apart
and cast away their cords from us."

4 He who sits in the heavens laughs;
the Lord holds them in derision.
5 Then he will speak to them in his wrath,
and terrify them in his fury, saying,
6 "As for me, I have set my King
on Zion, my holy hill."

7 I will tell of the decree:
The Lord said to me, "You are my Son;
today I have begotten you.
8 Ask of me, and I will make the nations your heritage,
and the ends of the earth your possession.
9 You shall break them with a rod of iron
and dash them in pieces like a potter's vessel."

10 Now therefore, O kings, be wise;
be warned, O rulers of the earth.
11 Serve the Lord with fear,
and rejoice with trembling.
12 Kiss the Son,
lest he be angry, and you perish in the way,
for his wrath is quickly kindled.
Blessed are all who take refuge in him.

STUDY HELP

- **Context**: Psalm 2 is called a ***"royal psalm"*** because it was used by the Davidic kings. It describes the coronation celebration of God's king in spite of the surrounding nations' complete rejection of that king. This Psalm instructs the idolatrous nations to repent from their rebellion against the Lord's anointed king and to bow down to Him in reverence.

- ***"his Anointed"*** – Every king under the Lord's authority was an "anointed one". On his coronation day the king was anointed as a symbolic act of special service to the Lord and His people (e.g. Solomon in 1 Kings 1:45).

- ***"burst their bonds...cast away their cords"*** – The surrounding nations desperately wanted to be released from the Lord's authority. Much like children who rebel against their parents' shepherding love, these nations considered the Lord's reign as oppressive rather than liberating.

- ***"derision"*** – In response to their audacious plan of rebellion God literally laughs at them. The enthroned God of heaven and earth sees through the ridiculousness and emptiness of their threats.

- ***"Zion"*** – was originally a Canaanite city conquered by David (2 Samuel 5:7). Zion later referred to the temple area and then to the entire city of Jerusalem. Here it represents the place upon which the Lord's King will reign for all eternity.

- ***"begotten"*** – This was a public declaration signifying that the king was a son of God the Father. Just as a son receives inheritance from his father, this son received the reign of the Father's Kingdom.

- ***"You shall break them with a rod of iron"*** – The nations opposing the Lord's King are a weak and feeble foe. They are like clay pots He can swiftly destroy with one strike from a rod of iron.

- ***"Serve the Lord with fear"*** – This is a call for those in rebellion to turn to reverence. It is a command for the creation to give respect to the Creator. And it is an act of love that calls them from the path of destruction to the place of refuge.

- ***"Kiss the Son"*** – Just as a kingdom citizen would gladly kiss the hand of a good and wise king, the nations are called to kiss the Lord's Anointed Son who brings life and all good things. This is an expression of submissive humility and affection for the King.

STUDY QUESTIONS

1. What posture are people taking before God in verses 1-3? Do you see any resemblance between these people and people today? Explain.

2. What does God's response to the plotting of the people (vv. 4-6) reveal about Him?

3. What does this psalm tell us about the place, identity, and action of God's King (vv. 4-9)?

4. What is the ultimate result of rejecting God's Anointed King (vv. 7-12)?

5. What is the proper response to the King of Zion (vv. 10-12)?

6. What is the hope for those who take refuge in God's King (v. 12)?

STUDY SUMMARY

Theologians consider David to be a "type," or foreshadow, of Christ. In this psalm, God is establishing His Son as the King of Zion and is putting Him above all other kings, rulers, and people. Anyone who stands against Him will surely and ultimately fail. But those who take refuge in Him will be blessed forever.

COACHING CONNECTION

The worshipful coach will humbly submit to God's Anointed King (Jesus), live with an awareness that everyone will give an account to Him, and seek to lead others to worship Him.

KEYS TO WINNING

▸ **VIDEO GUIDE AT KINGDOMSPORTS.ONLINE**

▸ AVOID FOOLISHNESS

A foolish person is someone that lacks good sense, judgment, and wisdom.

"WE WANT BAMA! WE WANT BAMA!" This has been the battle cry of many college football fan bases since 2009, only to be met with the disappointing results of their wishes. The 2021 college football season was no different.

As playoff time approached, some University of Cincinnati fans began to call out Alabama, hoping that's whom they would face in the playoffs. Cincinnati was undefeated at the time and clearly a good football team.

However, on January 1, 2022, it became equally clear that they had picked a fight with an opponent much bigger, faster, and stronger than them. Bama convincingly beat them 27-6. At best, if we might think of them as representing many today, Cincinnati's cries of valor were misplaced confidence. At worst, they were foolish and naive.

Naive and foolish postures are often seen in people who think too highly of themselves and too little of their opposition. The story is no different in Psalm 2.

In this psalm, we see a plot unfolding with the kings and rulers of the earth against the Lord and His Anointed. Their desire is to defeat the Lord and hold their throne and kingship forever. But we quickly learn that there will never be any fruitful results for anyone who stands against the Lord and His King.

1. Even though this posture against the Lord is foolish, how do you see that people are taking this same posture of foolishness against the Lord?

____

____

____

2. How are you tempted to take such a foolish posture before the Lord in your own life, particularly as a coach?

____

____

____

3. How can Psalm 2 fuel you to stay on course in pursuing your King's way

____

____

____

▸ ADORE THE KING

A lot can be discovered about someone as they confront opposition. Some will be revealed as cowardly; others will be revealed as bold. Some will be revealed as naive; others will be revealed as aware. Some will be revealed as weak; others will be revealed as strong.

Consider how the Lord responds to the opposition of the kings and rulers of the world:

> "He who sits in the heavens **laughs**;
>
> the Lord holds them in **derision…**"

It is obvious that the threats of the kings and rulers of the earth don't even begin to make God worrisome. The Lord laughs at their foolishness. He scorns at their threats. How can the Lord do this? How can He take these threats so lightly?

His power!

No one knows the depth of God's power but God Himself. In this moment we get a glimpse of just how powerful He is. In His power, God has set His King on Zion, the King who is above all kings. Every king of the earth can come against Him, but they will never measure up.

1. What does God's response to the threats of the nations tell you about Him?

____

____

____

____

2. How might knowing how powerful God is giving you hope in making your coaching King-centered?

____

____

____

____

3. Have you come to realize that the same King who saved you from your sins will condemn those who remain in theirs? If so, how does that reality impact the way you pray, live, and coach?

___

___

___

▸ ABIDE IN HUMILITY

As the psalmist says what the Lord will do for His son, he gives an exhortation to take the proper posture before the Lord: a posture of **humility.**

Humility is a misunderstood character trait. Some see it as the ability to act like they're not as good as they really are. Others see it as the willfulness to see themselves as terrible. But humility is really neither one.

Humility is one's modest opinion of one's own importance. For the worshipful coach, it is one's focus on Christ who is seeking for the good of others. It is Christ's mindset of selflessness "it's not about me." When you believe this to be true, you will stop comparing yourself with others by focusing only on Christ.

As a worshipful coach, why should your only focus be on Jesus? Here is what the psalmist tells us about the "King of Zion."

1. He's the Lord's Son (v. 7)
2. The nations are His heritage (v. 8)
3. Everything belongs to Him (v. 8)
4. No one can stand against Him (v. 9)

Consider this King's identity, the psalmist calls for a posture of humility. He calls for rulers and kings to be **wise** and **warned**, to understand what they're up against should they choose to oppose this King.

The psalmist calls us to **serve** the Lord with fear, **rejoice** with trembling, and **bow** before the Son, knowing that He is worthy and that anyone who comes against Him will desperately fail.

▸ QUICK TIME OUT

1. How would you describe your posture before King Jesus?

____

____

____

____

The opposite of humility is arrogance. It is an offensive display of superiority or self-importance. Such arrogance leads to superficial pride.

2. If you're being honest with yourself, how might arrogance have manifested itself in your life?

____

____

____

____

3. In what way/s might pride become a stumbling block for growth and success in your coaching career?

____

____

____

____

4. Because the chief mark of a worshipful coach is genuine humility before the Lord, what practices can you implement to grow in humble worship of the King (e.g., in relating to your athletes and staff, preparing for practices and competitions, balancing time between coaching and family, etc.)?

____

____

____

____

GAME CHANGER

In Psalm 2, we get a glimpse of the King that God places on the throne forever. There's no doubt that this Psalm is written to point us to King Jesus. Written over 1000 years before Jesus came to Earth, the reign of our King is surer than our very next breath. Consider Philippians 2:9-11:

> *"Therefore God has highly exalted him and bestowed on him the name that is above every name, so that at the name of Jesus every knee should bow, in heaven and on earth and under the earth, and every tongue confess that Jesus Christ is Lord, to the glory of God the Father."*

However, we cannot look at Jesus' reign without properly looking at the path He took to get there. Look at the previous verse in this same Philippians passage:

> *"And being found in human form, he humbled himself by becoming obedient to the point of death, even death on a cross."*

According to the above passage, Philippians 2:6, the road King Jesus took to His exalted position was the road of humility. The reason we can hope in King Jesus is that He suffered and died on our behalf. But death was not the end for this King.

This King rose from the grave with victory in hand for anyone who would trust in Him. This King is sitting on the throne ruling forever. This King owns everything. This King will make his enemies His footstool. This King guarantees salvation and victory for anyone who will run to Him.

This King offers us hope, because, in the words of the psalmist, *"blessed are all who take refuge in* ***Him.***" Praise Jesus for being our suffering, conquering, reigning King!

ONE BIG THING

What is the most significant lesson for you from this chapter?

IMPACT PRAYER

Father in heaven, You are far above all rulers and authorities on Earth. No one can successfully stand against You. Thank You for placing Your Anointed King on His throne forever. Help us never lose sight of His rule and reign. Help us never lose trust in His plan for us. Help us never lose faith that He is working all things for Your glory and for our good. Give us the strength to walk in confidence that our Savior and King is reigning for all eternity. Give us the boldness to use every moment we have, to expand His kingdom on the earth. For His praise, Amen.

KINGDOM COACHING

▸ PLAYBOOK FOR COACHING JESUS' WAY

A playbook is invaluable for your athletes to be at their best. It contains a detailed plan for their role on the team. Likewise, a Playbook for Coaching Jesus' Way is invaluable for you to be at your best. It contains a detailed plan for your role as a worshipful coach.

Jesus can only be "king" in your coaching life if you are committed to coaching His way. In Chapter One, we start to think of God's words in the Bible as our ultimate "coaching clinic."

Building on that, consider committing yourself to develop from the ultimate "coaching clinic" your personal Playbook for Coaching Jesus' Way. Eventually, you can glean principles from the entire life of Jesus (the biblical books of Matthew, Mark, Luke, and John) that will maximize you as a coach.

Here are just three examples:

1. Jesus enters the world (Luke 1:26-55 and 2:1-11): Enter the world of each person you lead with your mind and emotions as well as your physical presence.
2. Jesus selects disciples (Luke 6:12-16): In putting a leadership team together, select only those who are teachable and who are committed to learning and applying your values.
3. Jesus teaches His disciples (Matthew 5-7): Train your athletes in specific areas of conduct for both in and out of athletics. You can put an attractive label on such training (e.g., The Winning Way or The Champion's Way, etc.).

NOTES:

★ ★ ★

CHAPTER THREE

WORSHIPFUL COACHES

LOVE GOD'S GLORY

PSALM 19

STUDY STARTER

Tom Brady had just won his third Super Bowl at the age of 27. He was being interviewed on *60 minutes* by Steve Kroft. Consider their interaction:

KROFT: This whole experience—this whole upward trajectory—what have you learned about yourself? What kind of an effect does it have on you?

BRADY: Well, it put incredible amounts of pressure on me. When you feel like you're ultimately responsible for everyone and everything, even though you have no control over it, and you still blame yourself if things don't go right—I mean, there's a lot of pressure. A lot of times I think I get very frustrated and introverted, and there's times where I'm not the person that I want to be.

Why do I have three Super Bowl rings, and still think there's something greater out there for me? I mean, maybe a lot of people would say, "Hey man, this is what is." I reached my goal, my dream, my life. Me, I think: God, it's gotta be more than this. I mean this can't be what it's all cracked up to be. I mean I've done it. I'm 27. And what else is there for me?

KROFT: What's the answer?

BRADY: I wish I knew. I wish I knew. I mean I think that's part of me trying to go out and experience other things. I love playing football, and I love being a quarterback for this team, but, at the same time, I think there's a lot of other parts about me that I'm trying to find. I know what ultimately makes me happy are family and friends, and positive relationships with great people. I think I get more out of that than anything.

Tom's statement of emptiness is an honest reflection on our brokenness as humans. The word for "glory" in Psalm 19, which we will be looking at in this chapter, refers to the splendor and a display of praiseworthy greatness.

We are all made for glory, just not our own. We are made for the glory of God. As a coach, you can try your best to achieve and experience glory apart from Him, but you will inevitably fall short of the fullness that you long for.

Try as we may, our hearts will be restless until we find our rest in God. And our pursuits for glory will leave us empty until we direct all glory to the One who is worthy. So, now, let's turn our attention to the glory of God in Psalm 19 and see what He does to satisfy our longings and give rest to our hearts.

STUDY PASSAGE

19 TO THE CHOIRMASTER. A PSALM OF DAVID.

1 *The heavens declare the glory of God,*
and the sky above proclaims his handiwork.
2 *Day to day pours out speech,*
and night to night reveals knowledge.
3 *There is no speech, nor are there words,*
whose voice is not heard.
4 *Their voice goes out through all the earth,*
and their words to the end of the world.
In them he has set a tent for the sun,
5 *which comes out like a bridegroom leaving his chamber,*
and, like a strong man, runs its course with joy.
6 *Its rising is from the end of the heavens,*
and its circuit to the end of them,
and there is nothing hidden from its heat.

7 *The law of the Lord is perfect,*
reviving the soul;
the testimony of the Lord is sure,
making wise the simple;
8 *the precepts of the Lord are right,*
rejoicing the heart;
the commandment of the Lord is pure,
enlightening the eyes;
9 *the fear of the Lord is clean,*
enduring forever;
the rules of the Lord are true,
and righteous altogether.
10 *More to be desired are they than gold,*

even much fine gold;
sweeter also than honey
and drippings of the honeycomb.
11 *Moreover, by them is your servant warned; in keeping them there is great reward.* 12 *Who can discern his errors?*
Declare me innocent from hidden faults.

13 *Keep back your servant also from presumptuous sins;*
let them not have dominion over me!
Then I shall be blameless,
and innocent of great transgression.
14 *Let the words of my mouth and the meditation of my heart*
be acceptable in your sight,
O Lord, my rock and my redeemer.

STUDY HELP

- ***The glory of God in creation (vv. 1-6)*** – Creation is a resounding declaration to all people that God assuredly exists and is astonishingly magnificent. Every single day is a statement of God's glory. Like an award-winning singer, every nighttime sky exclaims the staggering depth and beauty of God's creative work. Like a world-class sprinter, the sun runs its daily race and enthusiastically points to the God of Heaven who alone is worthy of praise.
- ***The glory of God in special revelation (vv. 7-11)*** – God's Word is infinitely powerful and personally transformational. It is described as the law, the testimony, the precepts, the commandment, and the fear of the Lord. These varied descriptions are ways to help us understand and appreciate the glory of the Scriptures. God's Word is not simply a rulebook to be followed. It is the soul-reviving, wisdom-making, heart-rejoicing, eye-enlightening, righteousness-producing, endlessly-satisfying revelation of God that will endure forever.
- ***The glory of God in sanctification (vv. 12-14)*** – The worshiper who celebrates the glory of God in creation and special revelation also longs for personal transformation. It's one thing to see the glory of God with your eyes, it's another thing to experience it in your heart. This psalmist will not rest until his life displays the glory of God with the same zeal as creation and the Scriptures.

STUDY QUESTIONS

1. In what way/s does creation point us to the glory of God (verses 1-6)?

2. In verses 7-11, what are some attributes we learn about the Scriptures?

3. In verses 7-11, what are some things that the Law of the Lord accomplishes?

4. In verse 10, the Law of the Lord is compared to gold and honey. Describe how you would like the Law of the Lord—God's words in the Bible—to relate to you in coaching

5. From verses 12-14, how can you resonate with the psalmist's struggle against sin and desire to be free from transgression?

STUDY SUMMARY

God's glory is undeniable! His creation proclaims it. His Scriptures amplify it. And His worshipers get the privilege to see it, celebrate it, and be transformed by it.

COACHING CONNECTION

As a worshipful coach you have the privilege of expressing your sincere gratitude for the daily glories of God in creation, experiencing the life-transforming glory of His Scriptures, and being a living testimony of His glory to those around you.

KEYS TO WINNING

▸ **VIDEO GUIDE AT KINGDOMSPORTS.ONLINE**

▸ PRAISE GOD'S GLORY

Have you ever been at the beach, on the lake, driving down a back-road in the fall, or just watching a sunset in your backyard and been in awe at how beautiful God's creation is? Of course, you have.

The trees, the sky, the sun, the moon, the stars, the hills, the animals, the fish, the days, the seasons, the leaves, the ice, the snow, the heat, the steam, the fog, the grass, the dirt, the sand, the water, the cloud, the thunder, the lightning, the wind, and a million more wonders testify to the glory of God in creation.

There is no way to experience the marvels of this creation daily without beholding the glory of the Creator. Creation is meant to point us to God.

1. Describe two times in your life when you were in awe of the glory of God that you see in creation. How did those experiences reveal God's greatness?

____

____

____

____

2. List seven ways that God has displayed His glory to you over the last 24 hours.

____

____

____

____

▸ PURSUE GOD'S LAW

Oftentimes when we think about "law," it is in terms of the speed limit or having to stop for three seconds at a stop sign. Perhaps you might even associate "law" with officiating at your competitions. Usually, these laws feel like a burden and a nuisance rather than a help and delight.

However, this is not so with God's Law—His words in the Bible. God's Law is glorious. God's Law is perfect; it revives the soul. God's Law is sure; it makes the simple wise. God's Law is right; it rejoices the heart. God's Law is pure; it enlightens our eyes. God's Law is righteous; it endures forever.

As you might know, a five-tool player in baseball is one who can hit, hit with power, run, field, and throw. In other words, he can do it all. He can hit for average. He can hit home runs. He can steal bases. He can score from second on a base hit. He can field his position and he can make any throw necessary.

Statistically, there have been very few five-tool players in the game of baseball. It takes a rare combination of great athleticism and diligent, hard work to produce it. The beautiful thing about God's Law is that, if we pursue it, it will make us "five-tool" worshipers!

All Scripture is breathed out by God and profitable for teaching, reproof, correction, and training in righteousness (2 Timothy 3:16). Because that's true, God's Law is worth pursuing.

So, if you want to be a "five-tool" worshipful coach, in close fellowship with God, discipline yourself to pursue His Word each day. His law will shape your heart for Him and others, give you new desires for your athletes, help you know Him better, and satisfy your natural thirst for coaching glory.

1. In what ways have the blessings of God's Law, described in verses 7-11, affected your philosophy of coaching at this point in your life?

____

____

____

____

2. When we studied Psalm 1, we had a series of questions about being completely devoted to God's Word. And in that chapter's Kingdom Coaching section, we started to think of God's words in the Bible as our ultimate coaching clinic. Since then, in what way/s has God been using His words to maximize you as a leader?

____

____

____

____

▸ PERSIST IN GOD'S STRENGTH

When someone is training to develop a strong dead lift one of the first questions he needs to consider is, "Where does the power come from?"

If an athlete is training for a record-breaking dead lift but spends all his time on shoulder presses and bicep exercises, he won't see much success. To achieve his goal, a weightlifter must focus on the source of his power—his legs, hips, and back.

The same is true of a worshipful coach. The question we need to ask is, "Where does our power come from?" For our answer, we need to look no further than the words of Psalm 19. Consider *who* should receive the credit as you read verses 12-14:

> 12 *Who can discern his errors?*
> *Declare me innocent from hidden faults.*
> 13 ***Keep back your servant** also from presumptuous sins;*
> ***let them** not have dominion over me!*
> *Then I shall be blameless,*
> *and innocent of great transgression.*
> 14 ***Let the words** of my mouth and the meditation of my heart*
> *be acceptable in your sight,*
> ***O Lord, my rock and my redeemer.***

1. Who declares the worshiper innocent of hidden faults? ____________________________
2. Who keeps the worshiper from presumptuous sins? ________________________________
3. Who doesn't let sin have dominion over the worshiper? ____________________________
4. Who lets the words and meditations of the worshiper be acceptable?_________________
5. Are you looking to and resting in the power of God to strengthen you for all the challenges in your life?

____

____

____

6. The psalmist's response to the magnificence of God in the creation and the glory of God in the Scriptures is a personal plea for a life of holiness. God's greatness compels him

to want a life that reflects true gratitude and worship. So, he made some bold requests to the Lord. As a worshipful coach what requests would you like to make of the Lord as a response to His glory?

____

____

____

7. What a great feeling you would have if your athletes came to you with a plan to rid them of anything that is contrary to what you value as their coach. What can you do to rest more consistently in God to rid in you anything that is contrary to what He values?

____

____

____

GAME CHANGER

As a worshipful response to God's glory in creation and the Scriptures, the psalmist asked God to keep him from presumptuous sins and to declare him innocent and blameless. But the psalmist had the same problem that each of us have—inescapable, indwelling sin. Though the psalmist pursued God's law passionately and persistently he still fell short. And so do we.

But the good news is God knew we would never uphold his Law perfectly, so He sent someone to us who could…and did, Jesus Christ. Jesus lived a perfect life. He fulfilled every aspect of the Old Testament Law.

But more than that, Jesus endured the death that was most unfitting for Him to endure. Though he was perfect, He was crucified. And, in His crucifixion, God poured out His wrath on Him. However, three days after Jesus died, He rose in victory.

Every detail of Jesus' story matters. In His perfect life and death, God has completely fulfilled His Law. His wrath has been completely satisfied. And the people of God can walk in assurance because of Jesus' powerful resurrection.

You are not saved by anything you have done or will ever do. You are saved by the sufficient life, death, and resurrection of Christ. And as you walk in the newness of life, resting in the power of God, Christ, the Great Game Changer will transform you more and more into His image, and for God's glory.

ONE BIG THING

What is the most significant lesson for you from this chapter?

IMPACT PRAYER

Father in heaven, thank You for revealing Your glory to us through Your marvelous creation. Thank You for showing Your glory to us through the power of your Word. Thank You for Jesus, who has made it possible for us to be cleansed from our sins and to worship you authentically now and forever. Keep Your law on our hearts. Keep us from presumptuous sins and hidden faults. Empower us with Your Spirit as we walk in newness of life. In the name of Jesus, Amen.

KINGDOM COACHING

▸ YOUR TEAM AS GOD'S SHOWCASE

As we have seen in Psalm 19, the world is a showcase for God to display His glory—His praiseworthy activity and greatness. As a worshipful coach, who seeks God's glory instead of your own, your team—as part of God's world—can also be such a showcase.

You have already taken the first step in Chapter One by thinking of God's words in the Bible as your ultimate coaching clinic. In Chapter Two, you took the second step in starting to develop your Playbook for Coaching Jesus' Way.

Now, for the third step.

As you implement your Playbook for Coaching Jesus' Way, commit your team to be a showcase for others to see God's activity…anyway, He chooses to show Himself. If for no one else but your athletes, staff, along with you and your family.

For example, as you are committed to coaching Jesus' way, God might show Himself in giving His vision for the team, or in healing a relationship, or in developing a game plan… actually, in every detail of your practices and competitions. Pray for, and look for, God's activity.

So, as a worshipful coach, what's the purpose of your team?

To be a showcase for God's glory—His praiseworthy activity.

There is no greater glory than that!

NOTES:

___

___

___

___

___

★ ★ ★

CHAPTER FOUR

WORSHIPFUL COACHES

REMEMBER THE CROSS

PSALM 22

STUDY STARTER

We cannot truly live for the glory of Christ unless we live at the foot of the cross. Yet, we tend to forget the cross in our daily lives. Now if someone asks us about the cross, we can go and retrieve it at a moment's notice. We know right where it is whenever we feel like we need it.

Sadly, the cross can be like a vacuum cleaner. It stays in the closet until we need it to clean up something we've spilled or to prepare for a special occasion.

But contemplation of the cross is not for special occasions *only*. Contemplation of the cross is not for when we've messed up our lives *only*. Our lives are intended to be lived at the foot of the cross. When our eyes are fixed on the cross, we know how to *respond* to life, *proceed* with life, and *live* life.

Christ's death on the cross is not a peripheral issue or secondary theme. It is the central, most crucial element of the Christian life. Our English word "crucial" comes from the Latin word crux, which is "cross." Without the cross there is no Christian life.

Charles Spurgeon said that, in reading Psalm 22, we are about to tread on hallowed ground. "*We should read reverently, putting off our shoes from our feet, as Moses did at the burning bush. If there be holy ground anywhere in Scripture, it is in this psalm.*" This psalm had its initial fulfillment with King David, but it had its ultimate fulfillment with the true Son of David, Jesus Christ.

Psalm 22 is a Messianic Psalm–a psalm that deals with the person and work of Jesus Christ. There are 16 of them in the psalms. Specifically, Psalm 22 tells us about the crucifixion of the Messiah.

T. Ernest Wilson says this psalm "contains 33 items describing death by crucifixion. When we consider that this cruel and painful method of execution was invented many centuries later, it gives us a vivid illustration of the inspiration of Holy Scripture by the Spirit of God."

This psalm expresses the emotions of the Son of God as He was hanging on the cross, suspended in the air between Heaven and Earth. Ironically, the God in Heaven was rejecting Him and the people on Earth were rejecting Him. So, there was no more appropriate place for Him to be hanging.

This psalm is all about emotion, the feelings of Christ. We know that Jesus had previously experienced almost all the sinless emotions that a man can feel: joy, happiness, compassion, anger, grief, sorrow, weakness, and even fear at Gethsemane.

At Calvary, Jesus experienced one more emotion – utter despair! All that He had feared in the garden the night before came to fruition on the cross. In Psalm 22, we will enter His despair.

STUDY PASSAGE

22 TO THE CHOIRMASTER: ACCORDING TO THE DOE OF THE DAWN. A PSALM OF DAVID.

1 *My God, my God, why have you forsaken me?*
Why are you so far from saving me, from the words of my groaning?
2 *O my God, I cry by day, but you do not answer,*
and by night, but I find no rest.

3 *Yet you are holy,*
enthroned on the praises of Israel.
4 *In you our fathers trusted;*
they trusted, and you delivered them.
5 *To you they cried and were rescued;*
in you they trusted and were not put to shame.

6 *But I am a worm and not a man,*
scorned by mankind and despised by the people.
7 *All who see me mock me;*
they make mouths at me; they wag their heads;

[8] *"He trusts in the Lord; let him deliver him;*
let him rescue him, for he delights in him!"

[9] *Yet you are he who took me from the womb;*
you made me trust you at my mother's breasts.
[10] *On you was I cast from my birth,*
and from my mother's womb you have been my God.
[11] *Be not far from me,*
for trouble is near,
and there is none to help.

[12] *Many bulls encompass me;*
strong bulls of Bashan surround me;
[13] *they open wide their mouths at me,*
like a ravening and roaring lion.

[14] *I am poured out like water,*
and all my bones are out of joint;
my heart is like wax;
it is melted within my breast;
[15] *my strength is dried up like a potsherd,*
and my tongue sticks to my jaws;
you lay me in the dust of death.

[16] *For dogs encompass me;*
a company of evildoers encircles me;
they have pierced my hands and feet—
[17] *I can count all my bones—*
they stare and gloat over me;
[18] *they divide my garments among them,*
and for my clothing they cast lots.

[19] *But you, O Lord, do not be far off!*
O you my help, come quickly to my aid!
[20] *Deliver my soul from the sword,*
my precious life from the power of the dog!

21 Save me from the mouth of the lion!
You have rescued me from the horns of the wild oxen!

22 I will tell of your name to my brothers;
in the midst of the congregation I will praise you:
23 You who fear the Lord, praise him!
All you offspring of Jacob, glorify him,
and stand in awe of him, all you offspring of Israel!
24 For he has not despised or abhorred
the affliction of the afflicted,
and he has not hidden his face from him,
but has heard, when he cried to him.

25 From you comes my praise in the great congregation;
my vows I will perform before those who fear him.
26 The afflicted shall eat and be satisfied;
those who seek him shall praise the Lord!
May your hearts live forever!

27 All the ends of the earth shall remember
and turn to the Lord,
and all the families of the nations
shall worship before you.
28 For kingship belongs to the Lord,
and he rules over the nations.

29 All the prosperous of the earth eat and worship;
before him shall bow all who go down to the dust,
even the one who could not keep himself alive.
30 Posterity shall serve him;
it shall be told of the Lord to the coming generation;
31 they shall come and proclaim his righteousness to a people yet unborn,
that he has done it.

STUDY HELP

- *The Cry of the Condemned* **(vv. 1-18)** – In summary, these are the cries of one forsaken by God: You won't help me (1b). You won't answer me (1c-2). You never did to anyone else what you're doing to me (3-5). You let them humiliate me (6-8). You have alienated me (9-11). You have handed me over to bloodthirsty beasts (12-13). You have condemned me to death (14-18). Yet, in the midst of his forsakenness, he remembers the holy character and loyal love that God had demonstrated to him.

- *The Call for Help* **(vv. 19-21)** – The desperate man cries out one last time. But this time he calls upon the **name** of the Lord ("O LORD"), the **character** of the Lord ("O you my help"), and the **power** of the Lord ("Save me"). His knowledge of God inspires his plea to God. In the midst of his deep despair, he relies upon what he knows about the goodness and greatness of God. Because God has forsaken him, only God is able to deliver him. So he cries out from despair with hope in the only One who can rescue him.

- *The Celebration of Deliverance* **(vv. 22-31)** – In summary, this is the celebration cry: Praise God for He answered with deliverance (22-24). Everyone shall rejoice in His marvelous rescue (25-28). The entire Kingdom will celebrate His victorious work (29-31). Notice the expansive impact of the Lord's accomplishment: the prosperous worship Him, the dying bow down to Him, the new generation serves Him, and His righteousness is proclaimed to a people yet unborn.

STUDY QUESTIONS

1. In the first section of this psalm (vv. 1-18), David feels forsaken by God as he prays and sees no answer from God. Yet in the midst of his suffering, he remembers and recalls the things he knows about God. What are three of those things?

2. Matthew 27:45-46, *Now from the sixth hour there was darkness over all the land until the ninth hour. And about the ninth hour Jesus cried out with a loud voice, saying, "Eli, Eli, lema sabachthani?* That is, *My God, my God, why have you forsaken me?* Why did Jesus have to experience this?

3. In the second section of this psalm (vv. 19-21) David uses four graphic dangers (the sword, the dog, the lion, the wild oxen) to describe his desperation and imminent death. His situation is humanly hopeless. So, what does David say or do at this most crucial moment?

4. Matthew 27:50, *And Jesus cried out again with a loud voice and yielded up His Spirit.* David was a sinner. Jesus was sinless. David made vows that he did not keep. Jesus always kept His word. David broke the law. Jesus fulfilled it completely.

Yet, when David cried out for help God rescued Him. When Jesus cried out for help, He was left on the cross to suffer and die. Why was Jesus left on the cross to die even though He was the true and better king?

____

____

____

5. In the third section of this psalm (vv. 22-31) David praises the Lord and encourages the people of Israel to celebrate Him. In experiencing God's rescuing grace, how have you responded?

____

____

____

6. About Jesus' death on the cross, we learn: *For you were slain, and by your blood you ransomed people for God from every tribe and language and people and nation.* (Revelation 5:9)

Though Jesus was not rescued from death, His resurrection secured victory over death. It is only through His conquering work that people from all places on the Earth will "turn to the Lord" and celebrate Him.

Psalm 22, takes us from the valley of despair to the height of celebration. What does this reveal to us about the depth of sin and the power of grace?

____

____

____

____

7. How might Psalm 22 give you God's perspective for dealing with any major setback in your coaching seasons?

____

____

____

STUDY SUMMARY

David's suffering in Psalm 22 is a shadow of the suffering of Jesus, a "preview" of it. Though David finds grace and is delivered, Jesus suffered death. Then He victoriously rose so we could be delivered, resulting in our praise of God and His glory.

COACHING CONNECTION

As a worshipful coach, what Jesus did for you on the cross can motivate you in working with your athletes and fellow coaches.

KEYS TO WINNING

▶ **VIDEO GUIDE AT KINGDOMSPORTS.ONLINE**

▶ REST IN THE LORD

In this Psalm we see the suffering of David on display. He goes into detail about how those around him have scorned and despised him. As you look deeper you see the cause of much of this suffering: his trust in the Lord. People despised him for his faith in the Lord.

What was true for David is also true today. The world despises those who trust in the Lord. We must not expect our experience on earth to be different from David's. Jesus Himself knew this to be true, look at his words in the Gospel of John:

> *"If the world hates you, know that it has hated me before it hated you.*
> *If you were of the world, the world would love you as its own;*
> *but because you are not of the world, but I chose*
> *you out of the world, therefore the world hates you." (John 15:18-19)*

As a worshiper of God and follower of Christ, you can expect to be hated by the world. You will be mocked, ridiculed, and despised. Just as David, and just as Christ, you will be persecuted by the world. And just as David, and just as Christ, you must resist the world, knowing your hope is in the Lord, and He will never fail.

1. How have you seen and felt persecution from the world in your life because of your allegiance to Jesus? How have you rested in God even in despair?

2. In what scenarios do you see yourself having the most trouble resisting the world's pressure and resting in the Lord's peace? What steps can you take to grow in this?

▸ REMEMBER THE LORD

Though we've seen the suffering of David on display, we can't stop there. It's really important to see how David responds to this suffering. Throughout this whole psalm, every time David speaks to his suffering, look at what he says as he transitions to thinking about the Lord:

> Verse 3 - *"Yet* **you** *are holy"*
>
> Verse 9 - *"Yet* **you** *are he who took me from the womb"*
>
> Verse 19 - *"But* **you,** *O Lord, do not be far off! O you my help"*

David responds to the persecution of the world by remembering the Lord. David remembers the Lord in specific ways and there is a lot to learn from him.

1. David remembers **who** the Lord is. This is really the root of all David is able to say. The first thing David calls to mind is that God is HOLY and God is KING. He is set apart and faithful, and He is ruler over all.

2. David remembers **what** the Lord has done. David reminds himself that those who came before him placed their hope in God, and He didn't fail them.

3. David also remembers the work God has done in his own life. He remembers that God created him in his mother's womb and has never left or forsaken him. So, he know that God is able to deliver him from evil.

   David remembers **why** we turn to the Lord. In verses 19-21, we see from David why he can faithfully cry out to God as his first and only option: because God is His help. God is all-powerful and sovereign. If he didn't care about us, this would not be good news. But because God cares deeply for us, we can run to Him with hope.

1. In remembering the Lord, what might be ways that the Lord has shown Himself to be faithful to you?

____

____

____

2. In what areas of coaching do you struggle to remember the Lord the most (e.g., practices, competitions, winning, losing, injuries, attitudes, family life, etc.)?

____

____

____

▸ RESPOND WITH WORSHIP

Psalm 22 asks the question "Why?" "My God, my God, why have you forsaken me?" But psalm doesn't give the answer.

However, in 2 Corinthians 5:21, Paul does give the answer: "For He made Him who knew no sin *to be sin* for us, that we might become the righteousness of God in Him."

Why did God forsake His Son on the cross? Because of you and me! God imputed the guilt of our sins onto Jesus Christ *in order* to impute the merit of Christ's righteousness onto us.

God put the guilt of our lying, cursing, adultery, idolatry, gluttony, slander, hatred, jealousy, and selfishness onto Jesus Christ. He credited our sins onto Jesus' account. God condemned His Son in our place and Jesus Christ took ownership of all our guilt. Wow!

When Jesus cried out on the cross, "My God, My God, why have You forsaken Me?" He was screaming the scream of the damned for us. On the cross that day, the Father punished His sinless Son as if He were the guilty sinner that you and I are. The Father put the full weight of His righteous wrath onto His Son.

On the cross, Jesus experienced God's condemnation for us. And because He did, Heaven awaits those of us who have turned from our sin and trust Him for our salvation. This is radical, endless, unimaginable love.

Considering this amazing love…

1. What you should KNOW?

____

____

____

2. What you should FEEL?

____

____

____

3. What you should DO?

____

____

____

GAME CHANGER

In this Psalm, David endures deep suffering and expresses the feeling of forsakenness by God. Consider His words again:

> *"For dogs encompass me;*
> *a company of evildoers encircles me;*
> *They have pierced my hands and feet–*
> *I can count all my bones–*
> *They stare and gloat over me;*
> *They divide my garments among them,*
> *and for my clothing they cast lots."*

Though God did not really forsake David, nor were his hands and feet pierced, that's how he felt. On the other hand, Jesus actually did endure each of those things as He hung on the cross. His hands and feet were pierced, He was mocked, His garments were divided and taken by soldiers, and He was forsaken by God. Jesus suffered and died on the cross, enduring the wrath of God. Because of the blood of Christ that was shed, all people of all nations can know and worship God. Because of Christ's suffering on the cross and victory over the grave, we can be transferred from death to life and live as worshipers of Christ. He is the ultimate Game-Changer and the one true King.

ONE BIG THING

What is the most significant lesson for you from this chapter?

____

____

____

____

____

IMPACT PRAYER

Father in heaven, though the world will come against us, we can rest in knowing You are for us. What Jesus suffered on the cross demonstrates the depth of Your love for us. Help us to rest in Your love, remember Your faithfulness, and respond in worship. In the name of Jesus, Amen.

KINGDOM COACHING

▸ COACHING AS AN EXPRESSION OF YOUR LOVE FOR CHRIST

In your mind, when you are attending the ultimate coaching clinic each time you read in your Bible, and with your commitment for your athletes to be a showcase for God's glory, you are ready to maximize your motivation to daily implement your *Playbook for Coaching Jesus' Way.*

Jesus told His first followers, "If you love me, you will keep my commandments" (John 14:15).

The Greek word for "if" in Jesus' statement is a conditional "if," meaning a person's actions will show whether the statement is true." Jesus was telling His followers they will express their genuine love for Him by carrying out His commandments.

When you consider Jesus' love for you—having demonstrated it on the cross by making the payment for your sin—you can express your love for Him by carrying out His commandments.

How? By implementing your *Playbook for Coaching Jesus' Way.*

Moment by moment. Day by day.

As an expression of your love for Him and for what He did for you on the cross.

★ ★ ★

CHAPTER FIVE

WORSHIPFUL COACHES

EXPERIENCE RESTORATION

PSALM 51

STUDY STARTER

To understand and appreciate the force of Psalm 51, we must first understand the context in which it was penned. So, take a moment to read the following historical account of King David's sin against God.

In the spring of the year, the time when kings go out to battle, David sent Joab, and his servants with him, and all Israel. And they ravaged the Ammonites and besieged Rabbah. But David remained at Jerusalem.

It happened, late one afternoon, when David arose from his couch and was walking on the roof of the king's house, that he saw from the roof a woman bathing; and the woman was very beautiful. And David sent and inquired about the woman. And one said, "Is not this Bathsheba, the daughter of Eliam, the wife of Uriah the Hittite?" So David sent messengers and took her, and she came to him, and he lay with her. (Now she had been purifying herself from her uncleanness.) Then she returned to her house. And the woman conceived, and she sent and told David, "I am pregnant."

So David sent word to Joab, "Send me Uriah the Hittite." And Joab sent Uriah to David. When Uriah came to him, David asked how Joab was doing and how the people were doing and how the war was going. Then David said to Uriah, "Go down to your house and wash your feet." And Uriah went out of the king's house, and there followed him a present from the king. But Uriah slept at the door of the king's house with all the servants of his lord, and did not go down to his house. When they told David, "Uriah did not go down to his house," David said to Uriah, "Have you not come from a journey? Why did you not go down to your house?" Uriah said to David, "The ark and Israel and Judah dwell in booths, and my lord Joab and the servants of my lord are camping in the open field. Shall I then go to my house, to eat and to drink and to lie with my wife? As you live, and as your soul lives, I will not do this thing." Then David said to Uriah, "Remain here today also, and tomorrow I will send you back." So Uriah remained in Jerusalem that day and the next. And David invited him, and he ate in his presence and drank, so that he made him drunk. And in the evening he went out to lie on his couch with the servants of his lord, but he did not go down to his house.

In the morning David wrote a letter to Joab and sent it by the hand of Uriah. In the letter he wrote, "Set Uriah in the forefront of the hardest fighting, and then draw back from him, that he may be struck down, and die." And as Joab was besieging the city, he assigned Uriah to the place where he knew there were valiant men. And the men of the city came out and fought with Joab, and some of the servants of David among the people fell. Uriah the Hittite also died. Then Joab sent and told David all the news about the fighting. And he instructed the messenger, "When you have finished telling all the news about the fighting to the king, then, if the king's anger rises, and if he says to you, 'Why did you go so near the city to fight? Did you not know that they would shoot from the wall? Who killed Abimelech the son of Jerubbesheth? Did not a woman cast an upper millstone on him from the wall, so that he died at Thebez? Why did you go so near the wall?' then you shall say, 'Your servant Uriah the Hittite is dead also.'"

So the messenger went and came and told David all that Joab had sent him to tell. The messenger said to David, "The men gained an advantage over us and came out against us in the field, but we drove them back to the entrance of the gate. Then the archers shot at your servants from the wall. Some of the king's servants are dead, and your servant Uriah the Hittite is dead also." David said to the messenger, "Thus shall you say to Joab, 'Do not let this matter displease you, for the sword devours now one and now another. Strengthen your attack against the city and overthrow it.' And encourage him."

When the wife of Uriah heard that Uriah her husband was dead, she lamented over her husband. And when the mourning was over, David sent and brought her to his house, and she became his wife and bore him a son. But the thing that David had done displeased the Lord And the Lord sent Nathan to David. He came to him and said to him, "There were two men in a certain city, the one rich and the other poor. The rich man had very many flocks and herds, but the poor man had nothing but one little ewe lamb, which he had bought. And he brought it up, and it grew up with him and with his children. It used to eat of his morsel and drink from his cup and lie in his arms, and it was like a daughter to him. Now there came a traveler to the rich man, and he was unwilling to take one of his own flock or herd to prepare for the guest who had come to him, but he took the poor man's lamb and prepared it for the man who had come to him."

Then David's anger was greatly kindled against the man, and he said to Nathan, "As the

Lord lives, the man who has done this deserves to die, and he shall restore the lamb fourfold, because he did this thing, and because he had no pity."

Nathan said to David, "You are the man! Thus says the Lord, the God of Israel, 'I anointed you king over Israel, and I delivered you out of the hand of Saul. And I gave you your master's house and your master's wives into your arms and gave you the house of Israel and of Judah. And if this were too little, I would add to you as much more. Why have you despised the word of the Lord, to do what is evil in his sight? You have struck down Uriah the Hittite with the sword and have taken his wife to be your wife and have killed him with the sword of the Ammonites. Now therefore the sword shall never depart from your house, because you have despised me and have taken the wife of Uriah the Hittite to be your wife.' Thus says the Lord, 'Behold, I will raise up evil against you out of your own house. And I will take your wives before your eyes and give them to your neighbor, and he shall lie with your wives in the sight of this sun. For you did it secretly, but I will do this thing before all Israel and before the sun.'" David said to Nathan, "I have sinned against the Lord." And Nathan said to David, "The Lord also has put away your sin; you shall not die. Nevertheless, because by this deed you have utterly scorned the Lord, the child who is born to you shall die." Then Nathan went to his house. – 2 Samuel 11-12

STUDY PASSAGE

51 TO THE CHOIRMASTER: A PSALM OF DAVID, WHEN NATHAN THE PROPHET WENT TO HIM, AFTER HE HAD GONE IN TO BATHSHEEBA.

1 *Have mercy on me, O God,*
according to your steadfast love;
according to your abundant mercy
blot out my transgressions.
2 *Wash me thoroughly from my iniquity,*
and cleanse me from my sin!

3 *For I know my transgressions,*
and my sin is ever before me.

[4] *Against you, you only, have I sinned*
and done what is evil in your sight,
so that you may be justified in your words
and blameless in your judgment.
[5] *Behold, I was brought forth in iniquity,*
and in sin did my mother conceive me.
[6] *Behold, you delight in truth in the inward being,*
and you teach me wisdom in the secret heart.

[7] *Purge me with hyssop, and I shall be clean;*
wash me, and I shall be whiter than snow.
[8] *Let me hear joy and gladness;*
let the bones that you have broken rejoice.
[9] *Hide your face from my sins,*
and blot out all my iniquities.
[10] *Create in me a clean heart, O God,*
and renew a right spirit within me.
[11] *Cast me not away from your presence,*
and take not your Holy Spirit from me.
[12] *Restore to me the joy of your salvation,*
and uphold me with a willing spirit.

[13] *Then I will teach transgressors your ways,*
and sinners will return to you.
[14] *Deliver me from bloodguiltiness, O God,*
O God of my salvation,
and my tongue will sing aloud of your righteousness.
[15] *O Lord, open my lips,*
and my mouth will declare your praise.
[16] *For you will not delight in sacrifice, or I would give it;*
you will not be pleased with a burnt offering.
[17] *The sacrifices of God are a broken spirit;*
a broken and contrite heart, O God, you will not despise.

18 *Do good to Zion in your good pleasure;*
build up the walls of Jerusalem;
19 *then will you delight in right sacrifices,*
in burnt offerings and whole burnt offerings;
then bulls will be offered on your altar.

STUDY HELP

Restore me personally (vv. 1-12)

- David asks for forgiveness (1-2)

  "abundant mercy" – a wealth of love; riches of compassion. Picture a treasure chest overflowing with forgiveness, mercy, love, grace, kindness, generosity.

  "blot out" – wipe clean; wipe out, annihilate.

- David confesses his sin (3-6)

  "transgressions" – crimes; offenses concerning property. David saw his sin as a crime against God, not merely a mistake.

  "Against you, you only, have I sinned" – David knew full-well that he had sinned against Bathsheeba, Uriah, their families, and the entirety of his kingdom. But his emphasis in this confession is the reality that at the deepest level, his sin is against God Himself.

  "I was brought forth in iniquity" – This confession is not an indication that David was conceived in an immoral relationship. It is a confession that all humans are conceived, born, and live in a state of sinful brokenness. Sin was ingrained in David's DNA.

- David pleads for cleansing (7-9)

  "hyssop" – herb with purging qualities; Assyrian or Egyptian plant. It was mentioned in the Bible for its cleansing effect in connection with plague, leprosy and chest ailments and symbolically in cleansing the soul.

- David prays for revival (10-12)

  "Take not your Holy Spirit from me" David enjoyed a special anointing of the Holy Spirit because he was God's king. As a young man, David endured the dark deeds of King Solomon after God removed His special anointing from him. So David pled with God to not take that same anointing from him.

Use me corporately (vv. 13-19)

- David commits to praise God publicly (13-15)

  "bloodguiltiness" – the shedding of blood. In other words, David pleads for God not to shed his blood, even though he is guilty and deserves it.

- David commits to love God inwardly (16-17)

  "broken and contrite heart" – completely shattered, smashed, and crushed. God despises one who approaches Him with the delusion of wholeness or completeness, but draws near to those who acknowledge they are broken.

- David commits to worship God ceremonially (18-19)*"altar"* – the platform on which offerings were made to God.

STUDY QUESTIONS

1. On which attributes of God does David stake his request for forgiveness (vv. 1-2)?

___

___

___

2. What does David mean in stating that he only sinned against God when others were clearly hurt (v. 4)?

___

___

___

___

3. David makes some radical requests of God for a man who has sinned so dramatically. What do these audacious petitions tell us about David's confidence in the character and love of God (vv. 7-12)?

4. With which request of David's do you identify with the most? Why?

5. In verses 13-15, forgiveness from the Lord created an outward change in David. What did he commit to do?

6. What might be the impact if you made a similar commitment to your athletes?

7. Considering possible restrictions on what you are allowed to do in your coaching role, how can you make a similar commitment?

8. Though we tend to grade sin on the curve, God is offended by all of it, not just adultery and murder. What is an example of repentance in your life?

____

____

____

STUDY SUMMARY

David sinned terribly against God, but out of God's love and mercy, He forgave all David's transgressions and iniquities. David rejoiced in forgiveness, worshiped God, and, in thankfulness, declared God's love to those around him.

COACHING CONNECTION

As a worshipful coach, you can confess your sins to God, be fully cleansed and restored, then, in thankfulness, declare God's love to those around you.

KEYS TO WINNING

▶ **VIDEO GUIDE AT KINGDOMSPORTS.ONLINE**

▶ RECOGNIZE

David wrote this psalm after committing sins that most people would consider to be the ultimate bad—adultery and murder. People are often blind to their own sinfulness. But once God used Nathan to open David's eyes, the king clearly saw his sin. In this chapter, David recognizes three crucial realities that lead him to repentance

The Character of God *- Throughout this psalm, David is aware of God's authority and rule. So, he knows he has rejected God's authority. However, at the beginning of the chapter, David recognizes God's mercy and love. This recognition gave David confidence in his repentance.*

The Nature of Man *- In almost all the first half of the psalm, David is recognizing his sinful nature, not only his sin. He knows that nothing good comes from within himself. He also knows that only God can cleanse his heart and remove his sin.*

The Need for Forgiveness *- Considering knowing who God is as well as knowing who he himself is, David, is certain that forgiveness is a necessity. He has fallen short of the standard that God had put in place, and he knows that his falling is serious and requires action.*

1. Which of David's three recognitions is the hardest for you, and why?

____

____

____

2. Which is the easiest, and why?

____

____

____

▸ REPENT

As we read David's words, we can feel his anguish over his sin. David's heart was broken because he had failed to faithfully obey His Father and Lord.

1. How do you feel when you realize you're walking in sin against your Father?

____

____

2. What might your feeling tell you about how you view God and his righteous commands?

____

____

____

3. Why is it necessary for you, as a worshipful coach, to be repentant before God?

David knew that his sin was heinous, but he also knew that God's love was greater than his sin. So, he cried out, asking God to have mercy on him. Being confident in God's love, David ran to God with a heart of repentance. God did show him mercy and forgave him.

4. How does knowing that God loves you influence your own repentance?

5. What might you do to more consistently live and coach in awe of God?

6. If you have ever played for a coach who was too arrogant to admit he/she was wrong, how did his/her attitude affect your relationship with that coach?

7. How can you develop a readily-repentant humility that honors the Lord and avoids this type of never-wrong arrogance?

▸ RECITE

In the second half of this psalm, David declares what he will do once the Lord "restores to him the joy of his salvation." He will recite, or proclaim, the excellencies of the Lord to all people. It's part of our nature to elevate to others what we think is deserving of praise.

Think about a fantastic movie you have seen. Afterward, how often did you tell someone how wonderful that movie was? How often did you recite, or proclaim, to others the acting prowess, the plot twist, and the climax of the movie? Probably a lot! We recite to others what means a lot to us.

David did, too. From personal experience, he knew that God was worthy of all worship and praise. He couldn't help but proclaim God's grace and forgiveness to others.

1. How would you describe your present desire to recite, or proclaim, God's grace and forgiveness to others whom God has placed in your life?

____

____

____

2. If you have ever shared that hope with one of your fellow coaches or players, describe what happened.

____

____

____

3. On a scale of 1-10, how would you rate your personal evangelism, and why did you give yourself that rating?

____

____

____

4. How can you develop more boldness in reciting, or proclaiming, the Lord's grace and forgiveness to those around you?

____

____

____

GAME CHANGER

Psalm 51, is a beautiful portrait of authentic repentance and the faithful mercy of the Lord. David's pleas to God in verses 9-12 come from deep in his heart of personal experience:

> *"Hide your face from my sins,*
> *and blot out all my iniquities.*
> *Create in me a clean heart, O God,*
> *and renew a right spirit within me.*
> *Cast me not away from your presence,*
> *and take not your Holy Spirit from me.*
> *Restore to me the joy of your salvation,*
> *and uphold me with a willing spirit."*

For a moment, let's consider how God would restore us, daily, in our fellowship with Him. We will be thinking of David's pleas as our own pleas. When we consider what David is asking God to do, our question is: How will God restore us? The short answer is JESUS.

If you run to Jesus, God will blot out your iniquities because Jesus paid for them on the cross.

If you run to Jesus, God will give you a clean heart and fill you with His Holy Spirit.

If you run to Jesus, God will not cast you out from His presence, but will always give you complete access to Him.

If you run to Jesus, God will always restore the joy of salvation to you because Jesus' blood is sufficient to cover all sin.

True repentance is found only in running to Christ. Have you run to Him to save your soul? Are you running to Him to constantly wash you clean with His blood? His blood is sufficient to wash even the worst of sinners.

ONE BIG THING

What is the most significant lesson for you from this chapter?

IMPACT PRAYER

Father in heaven, thank You for your love and faithfulness to forgive us through the blood of Jesus. Give us the same heart of David that feels the weight of sin and allow us to wholeheartedly repent of our sins every time we approach Your throne. Use us to be the voice that proclaims Your glory to our families, athletes, and the rest of the world. In the name of Jesus, Amen.

KINGDOM COACHING

▸ THINK OF YOUR TEAM AS GOD'S FAMILY

One dictionary definition of family is a group of people who are generally not blood-related but who share common attitudes, interests, or goals, and frequently live together.

That's your team. Or at least it is for two to three hours a day during the season. However, in thinking of your team as God's family, we are talking about more than just athletes and coaches being together with common interests.

We're talking about possible restorations.

Here's the thing. Everyone is somewhere in relation to God, even an avowed atheist. God is the Designer and Creator of every person even if they don't acknowledge Him.

By thinking of your team as God's family, as you yield to Him, He will use you to help each family member develop and experience a close bond with God, including restoring a broken relationship with Him.

Let's say that one of your athletes consistently has a rotten attitude. Most likely, his/her attitude flows out of their disconnect with God. Your role is to get at the root cause of their bad attitude…and that is to help them initially connect with God, the Head of the "family," or be restored in their broken relationship with Him.

The bottom line?

As you think of your team as God's Family, you will be more sensitive to how each family member is relating to the Head of the family…and how you might help restore those in a broken relationship with Him.

Just as God restored David.

NOTES:

CHAPTER SIX

WORSHIPFUL COACHES

PURSUE GOD'S PRESENCE

PSALM 84

STUDY STARTER

There is a Hall of FAITH in the Bible. It's found in Hebrews 11. That chapter chronicles the faith of those who believed in the Lord through difficult circumstances. If you haven't read it in a while, it would be good to refresh your mind. God's Hall of Faith will encourage and inspire you to keep believing in—relying on—the Lord no matter what you're going through.

Although there is a Hall of FAITH in the Bible, there is *no* Hall of FAME. There is no list of spiritual superheroes. If you are on the hunt for a spiritual superhero, you will be disappointed with the men and women of the Bible. Except for Jesus, not one of them lived a spotless life.

Adam was passive. Noah was a drinker. Abraham was a liar. Sarah was a manipulator. Lot was a compromiser. Jacob was a deceiver. Job was arrogant. Moses was hot-tempered. Gideon was idolatrous. Samson was lustful. David was an adulterer. Solomon was hedonistic. Elijah was self-centered. Jonah was a racist.

Isaiah was foul-mouthed. Jeremiah was a complainer. Matthew was a tax collector who exploited his own people for financial gain. Martha was a diligent homemaker so busy with her duties that she left no time for worship. Thomas was a doubter. James and John were explosive and selfishly ambitious.

Peter was a loyalist who said to Jesus, "I love you. I will never deny You." Then hours later, in the face of personal danger, he testified, "I don't know the man!" Even the Apostle Paul had warts. At times he could be seen as an intolerant leader (in his disapproval of John Mark) and a name-caller (as he stood before the high priest).

So why do we look at some of these people as heroes? It's certainly not because they were perfect. What we see in them is not perfection but passion. Many had a "superhero" passion for God and a relentless desire to worship Him.

Consider David's heart in Psalm 27: "One thing have I asked of the Lord, that will I seek after: that I may dwell in the house of the Lord and to inquire in his temple...You have said, 'Seek my face.' My heart says to you, 'Your face Lord, do I seek.'"

Consider Peter's heart in John 13, "Peter said to him, 'You shall never wash my feet.' Jesus answered, 'If I do not wash you, you have no share with me.' Simon Peter said to him, 'Lord, not my feet only but also my hands and my head!'"

Consider Paul's heart in Philippians 3: "that I may know him and the power of his resurrection, and may share his sufferings, becoming like him in his death, that by any means possible I may attain the resurrection of the dead."

We admire David, Peter, and Paul because they had a passion to worship God beyond the superficial. Despite their many struggles and failures, they were not content to swim in the shallow end of the worship pool. Instead, they wanted to tread the deep waters of knowing and experiencing God's greatness, glory, and grace!

Those are the worshipers whom God desires! And that is the quality of worshiper that we read about in Psalm 84. In this psalm, the psalmist passionately longs to travel to Jerusalem and worship the Lord with greater intimacy and intensity. In this chapter, you will find that to be a genuine worshiper of God; you must be passionate about worship.

STUDY PASSAGE

84 TO THE CHOIRMASTER: ACCORDING TO THE GITTITH· A PSALM OF THE SONS OF KORAH·

1 *How lovely is your dwelling place,*
O Lord of hosts!
2 *My soul longs, yes, faints*
for the courts of the Lord;
my heart and flesh sing for joy
to the living God.
3 *Even the sparrow finds a home,*
and the swallow a nest for herself,

where she may lay her young,
at your altars, O Lord of hosts,
my King and my God.
4 *Blessed are those who dwell in your house,*
ever singing your praise! Selah

5 *Blessed are those whose strength is in you,*
in whose heart are the highways to Zion.[b]
6 *As they go through the Valley of Baca*
they make it a place of springs;
the early rain also covers it with pools.
7 *They go from strength to strength;*
each one appears before God in Zion.
8 *O Lord God of hosts, hear my prayer;*
give ear, O God of Jacob! Selah

9 *Behold our shield, O God;*
look on the face of your anointed!
10 *For a day in your courts is better*
than a thousand elsewhere.
I would rather be a doorkeeper in the house of my God
than dwell in the tents of wickedness.
11 *For the Lord God is a sun and shield;*
the Lord bestows favor and honor.
No good thing does he withhold
from those who walk uprightly.
12 *O Lord of hosts,*
blessed is the one who trusts in you!

STUDY HELP

We see three stages in the worshiper's desperation for God.

His DESIRE for the presence of God (vv. 1-4)

- Declaration about the LORD's house

  O Lord of Hosts - The psalmist uses this title four times in the psalm. What does it mean? The hosts are angelic beings that surround the Lord's heavenly throne and praise Him, carrying out God's sovereign will throughout the world. By calling God the Lord of Hosts, he is calling Him the self-existent, supreme commander of all the heavenly forces.

  Your dwelling place - This psalm uses a variety of terms to describe the place where God's abiding presence is. "Your dwelling place" is the tabernacle of God in the city of Jerusalem.

- Desperation for the LORD'S house
- Delight in the LORD's house

His JOY in the journey to God (vv. 5-8)

- Preparation for the journey

  Whose heart is set on highways to Zion - Though God's people are not always present in God's house, their hearts are fixed and focused on getting there.

- Progress in the journey

  Valley of Baca - In the journey to God's house, the Valley of Baca represents moments that are dry, difficult, and create a sense of desperation.

- Petition as he considers their journey

His TRUST in the goodness of God (vv. 9-12)

- Plea to God

  Your anointed - This is a reference to the King of Israel, the one specially anointed for this office. Though the psalmist possibly had David in mind, this ultimately points to The Anointed One–Jesus Christ.

- Privilege with God
- Protection with God

  The Lord God is a sun and shield - As a sun, the Lord gives heat for our hearts and light for our paths. As a shield, the Lord gives the provision of his presence and protection from the enemies.

- Peace with God

STUDY QUESTIONS

1. The psalmist starts by describing how his soul desires to be in the dwelling place of the Lord. What three verbal phrases in verse 2 demonstrate his passion to be in the Lord's presence?

2. This psalm gives us great insight into the character of God. But you must look for it through the lens of the worshiper's delight in God. In looking through that lens, what are at least three characteristics of God in this psalm that make Him worthy of worship?.

3. The psalmist describes those who are "blessed" three times (vv. 4, 5, 12). That means they are happy and whole. So, what are these blessed people doing?

4. Verse 10 gives us a view into the psalmist's heart. How does he compare life in the world to life in God's presence?

5. In verses 11-12, the Lord gives favor and honor to those who walk uprightly and trust Him. In being a worshipful coach walking upright and trusting God, how might God give you favor and honor?

6. How would you compare your hunger for God with your hunger for a successful sports season.

STUDY SUMMARY

This worshiper desperately longs to be in the LORD's house to enjoy His presence and express His praise.

COACHING CONNECTION

A worshipful coach pursues the Lord, above all else, to enjoy His presence in every detail of life, including every detail of coaching.

KEYS TO WINNING

▶ **VIDEO GUIDE AT KINGDOMSPORTS.ONLINE**

▶ LONG FOR LIFE WITH GOD

Imagine that you have been appointed to coach an elite team for an upcoming national competition. The only drawback is that you will be away from home for two months. At the start, you are full of excitement. But as time passes, you miss home and long for it each day.

Finally, the competition comes, your team does well, and you board a plane for home. Your longing is almost over. Upon landing, you take a cab home and excitedly burst through the front door shouting, "I'm home!" But no one else is.

How would you feel that you've made it "home" only to be greeted by an empty house? Those you love aren't there.

You didn't long for home because you couldn't stop dreaming about the architecture of your house or its many plants. For two months, you longed for home because it was full of the people you love and care for most. Home is not a building where you are; it's who you're with.

In Psalm 84, the worshiper longs to be in God's house because that's where God resides. He wants to be as close to God as possible. The psalmist had a radical desire to be at home with the Lord in the Lord's house.

1. How would you compare your longing to be in God's presence with the psalmist's longing to be in God's presence?

____

____

____

____

2. What about God makes you long to be with Him?

3. When you take time to think about it, what is it about God that would make you long to be with Him?

4. When you take time to think about it, what is it about God that would make you long to be with Him?

5. How might your awareness of being in God's presence affect your mindset during a competition in which you are winning? In which you are losing?

▸ LIVE IN THE STRENGTH OF GOD

Everyone depends on strength. We need mental strength to process our thoughts, solve problems, and make decisions. We need physical strength to walk, run, lift, compete, and speak.

So, from our own experience, we know that mental and physical strength is essential in living and coaching. But interestingly, this psalm teaches that spiritual strength, depending on the Lord and His strength, is also essential

1. On a scale of 1-10, rate your dependence on the Lord and His strength.

1	2	3	4	5	6	7	8	9	10

In verse 5, the Psalmist confirms the source of our spiritual strength. It does not come from within; it comes from the Lord. Therefore, anyone attempting to be spiritually strong without being completely dependent on the Lord will fail.

In speaking about Jesus in John 3:30, John the Baptist exclaims, *"he must increase, but I must decrease."* This should be the battle cry of anyone who wants to experience the Lord's strength: "He must increase, but I must decrease."

Now, here are four ways to help you experience the Lord's increasing and your decreasing:

A. Recognize that you are not strong.

B. Depend on the Holy Spirit to give you strength.

C. Look to God's Word for guidance and hope.

D. Focus on God's unwavering presence.

2. Of these four ways, which might need to focus on the most, and how will that be helpful?

____

____

____

____

____

In this life, a worshiper of God is a foreigner on Earth. God has redeemed you for eternal worship of Him. But you are still in this sin-cursed, messed-up world. So, as a worshipful coach, it's crucial that you keep in mind that this present world is not your home.

Fix your eyes on the Lord and rely on Him as your strength. As you journey toward God, your strength must be in Him and Him alone.

3. How might viewing yourself as a foreigner on Earth influence the way you coach?

____

____

____

____

4. Sports is a dog-eat-dog world. The weak get chewed up and spit out. How can you be successful as a God-increasing and self-decreasing coach in a world built on one's own strength?

____

____

____

____

▸ FEED YOUR DESIRE FOR GOD

As a worshipful coach, God has implanted a desire in your heart for Him. But your flesh—sinful nature—strongly resists that desire. It will keep trying to distract you from fixing your eyes on God and destroy your desire for Him.

You must be intentional in worshipping Him. Without the discipline of intentionality, your desire for God will be shallow, and your delight in His presence will be fleeting. One way to feed your desire for God is to commit yourself to the Row, the Circle, and the Chair.

> **The Row** = Sunday Morning Worship with the Church (referring to rows of seats for the worshipers).
>
> > Although you attend the worship service with other believers on Sunday morning, you prepare for it on Saturday night. Plan to take notes on the message to help you grow as a worshipful coach.

When the psalmist arrived at the temple, he would have joined other like-minded worshipers, greeters at the temple gate, servants inside the temple, Levites working hard, priests offering sacrifices, teachers explaining the Law, and many others carrying out the duties of corporate worship. But, as he longed for the presence of God, he was simultaneously longing for the people of God.

1. With the psalmist's experience in mind, why is gathering with God's people important each week?

____

____

____

____

The Circle = Small Groups studying God's Word and praying together (referring to a circle of believers).

Commit to a small group of believers with whom you will discuss the Word of God, deal with issues of theology and life, be accountable, and pray for one another.

2. How has *this* circle (studying *The Worshipful Coach*) affected your pursuit of God?

____

____

____

____

The Chair = One-on-One time with God each day.

Commit to a daily time with God during which you will read the Bible, meditate on what you read, and pray.

3. If there has been a time in your life when you were spending daily time in God's Word, how did that affect you as a coach, if at all?

____

____

____

____

GAME CHANGER

Psalm 84 leaves no doubt that dwelling in the house of the Lord is desirable above all things. But there is a problem. Dwelling in the house of the Lord requires perfect righteousness, and only God qualifies. Therefore, His holiness and our sinfulness cannot dwell together.

Even though we can never live a perfectly righteous life, Jesus did. The good news of Jesus is that God attributes Jesus' upright life to us when we trust in who Jesus is and what He has done for us on the cross. As the Son of God, He paid the penalty for our sins, a punishment that we deserved. Then Jesus rose to life on the third day.

If you believe in Him, you can dwell with Him because Jesus endured the death and punishment you deserve.

Your hope must not be in your own ability to earn a spot in God's house. Instead, all your hope must sit squarely on who Christ is, what He has done, and how He gives you access to God.

ONE BIG THING

What is the most significant lesson for you from this chapter?

IMPACT PRAYER

Father in Heaven, Your glory, holiness, righteousness, and faithfulness are just a few reasons You are worthy of worship. Thank You for Christ, who gives me full access to Your presence. Keep me from being caught up in worldly pursuits, knowing that I am a stranger on earth and that citizenship is with You in Heaven. Help me to pursue Your presence now and forevermore passionately. In the name of Jesus, Amen.

KINGDOM COACHING

Think of God's Presence in Each Practice and Competition.

From experience, we know what it's like *not* to be aware of God's presence. Our natural tendencies are on full display. And, unless we choose to be aware of God's presence, by default, we aren't…thanks to our sin nature.

But think for a moment what it might be like if you were as aware of God's presence as you are of your athletes practicing and competing. Or what it might be like in your coaching office if you were as aware of God's presence as you are of yourself or anyone else.

In Proverbs 15:3, we learn, "The eyes of the LORD are in every place, keeping watch on the evil and the good." And in Psalms 139:7, David asks, "Where shall I go from your Spirit? Or where shall I flee from your presence?" The answer is, "No place. You are everywhere at the same time!"

★ ★ ★

CHAPTER SEVEN

WORSHIPFUL COACHES

GIVE GOD PRAISE

PSALM 100

STUDY STARTER

Praising God is a natural part of worshipping Him. The act of praising is as natural for us as attending a sports event. We enjoy cheering on our favorite team, unlike the animal world.

In the Kentucky Derby, horses don't crowd behind the rails of Churchill Downs to cheer on their favorite in the race. In greyhound races, dogs don't bark for their hero. Bears don't jump up and down alongside the riverbank to cheer on Big Brown as he skillfully snatches a trout. And sharks don't give each other high-fins when Jaws consumes his biggest seal yet.

Animals aren't captivated by the talents and feats of their fellow animals.

But humans are!

For thousands of years, humans have been captivated by the talents and feats of their fellow humans. We gather to watch athletic prowess. We assemble in awe of musical talent. We travel far and wide to witness extraordinary achievements of...well, you name it.

God has made us different than animals. He has hardwired into each of us the capacity and desire to worship. Simply put, God made us for worship. Perhaps that's one reason we are so captivated by sports. We love to be amazed and in awe. We love to be dazzled by the best of the best.

In turn, we worship what awes and dazzles us. In sports, we give our highest praise to the athletes and teams that dazzle us the most. In music, we give the most plays to the musicians who delight us the most.

In Psalm 100, we look into the heart of a worshiper who will show us how to use our "hard-wired" desire to praise to connect with and praise God, the One who awes and dazzles us the most.

STUDY PASSAGE

100 A PSALM FOR GIVING THANKS.

[1] *Make a joyful noise to the Lord, all the earth!*

[2] *Serve the Lord with gladness!*

Come into his presence with singing!

[3] *Know that the Lord, he is God!*

It is he who made us, and we are his;

we are his people, and the sheep of his pasture.

[4] *Enter his gates with thanksgiving,*

and his courts with praise!

Give thanks to him; bless his name!

[5] *For the Lord is good;*

his steadfast love endures forever,

and his faithfulness to all generations.

STUDY HELP

- ***"Make a joyful noise"*** – a loud, public shout that signals a strong feeling or future action (e.g., blowing an instrument, shout of exuberance, shout of worship)
- ***"Serve"*** – can also be translated "worship." The two English terms come from the same Hebrew word, which means to expend considerable energy and intensity in a task or function. Worship is energetic and intense, not flippant or casual.
- ***"Gates"** and **"Courts"*** – These were the gates of the temple for God's people to enter His presence. The courts were open spaces and courtyards in the temple designed for the gathering of God's people to worship Him.

STUDY QUESTIONS

1. Action. List the seven instructive verbs given to the worshiper of God in this psalm.

2. Approach. In approaching the Lord, the psalmist also describes how to properly posture ourselves before Him (e.g., "with singing")—list as many of these postures as you can see.

3. Attributes. List as many character traits of God that you can see in this psalm.

4. Relationship. The authentic and close connection that a worshiper has with God is special. What are some phrases in this psalm that indicate this truth?

5. Passionate worship begins in the heart and becomes an outward expression of our praise to God for those things about Him of which we are in awe. What might a lack of genuine enthusiasm indicate about our relationship with God?

STUDY SUMMARY

God is incredibly good to His people. Therefore, the only appropriate response is enthusiastic praise from those who worship Him.

COACHING CONNECTION

If we are to liken our worship of God to our attendance at a sports event, we can think of our ovation as our praise of Him. Praise expresses our worship…even in the heat of competition.

KEYS TO WINNING

▶ **VIDEO GUIDE AT KINGDOMSPORTS.ONLINE**

▸ PRAISE THE LORD PASSIONATELY

Think of a time at any gathering for worship when someone's expression of praise made you uncomfortable. In Psalm 100, we see a worshiper who was so caught up in the glorious character of God that he realized his only proper response was enthusiastic, expressive, passionate praise.

So, let's talk about passion.

On a ten-point scale, with "10" being the most passionate, how much passion do you want your players to have for training, practicing, and competing? How about being on your team? Most likely, a "10" for everything, right? We want our athletes to have passion and express it in their training, practicing, and competing.

If we can see the value of having a passion for something as temporary as sports, we can easily understand why the God who created the universe out of nothing would want us to have passion in our praise of Him.

1. The dictionary defines passion as a powerful and compelling emotion or feeling. In one sentence, describe the passion you have to coach your team.

____

____

____

2. In one sentence, describe the passion you presently have for praising God.

____

____

____

▸ PRAISE THE LORD GLADLY

The Lord wants and deserves glad worshipers. He wants people who have joy—an attitude of gladness—in their relationship with Him. And you qualify. You have a lot to be glad about.

The Creator of the universe has also designed you exactly how He wanted. And, as a Christian, you no longer need to fear death. Instead, you have eternal life because of the Spirit of Christ in you. So, you can "praise the Lord gladly," full of joy and delight.

1. How might a lifestyle of praising the Lord gladly affect your family life?

____

____

____

____

2. How might a lifestyle of praising the Lord gladly affect your coaching?

____

____

____

____

▸PRAISE THE LORD MUSICALLY

In verse 2, the psalmist tells us to come into God's presence with singing.

Think back to the most exciting concert you ever attended. How did you feel when your favorite song began, and everyone sang along? How awesome was it to be lifting a song with thousands of people? Being all-in at a phenomenal concert is hard to beat.

God created music. In Psalm 100, He prioritizes our singing in praise of Him. Keeping in mind that musical praise is not about the quality of your voice but the condition of your heart, how might you regularly praise God with your singing?

____

____

____

▸WORSHIP THE LORD KNOWLEDGEABLY

Your knowledge of God's attributes will fuel your desire to praise Him. The deeper you go in your knowledge of God, the higher you can go in your worship of Him. So, here are a few of God's attributes you can etch in your mind.

God is **eternal**. He has no beginning or end.
God is **invisible**. No one has ever seen the totality of His essence.
God is **spirit**. He has no parts, size, or dimensions.
God is **unchangeable**. He is not like us.
God is **omniscient.** He knows everything.
God is **omnipresent**. He is everywhere.
God is **omnipotent**. He does what He wants.
God is **independent**. He doesn't need us.
God is **holy.** He is separate, sinless, and supreme.
God is **righteous.** He always does what is right.
God is **jealous**. He seeks to protect His own honor.
God is **perfect.** He possesses every excellent attribute.
God is **wise**. He always accomplishes the best possible goals.
God is **good.** All that He does is worthy of praise.

God is **love.** He passionately pursues the highest good of His people.

God is **beautiful.** He possesses every quality that is awesome, desirable, and pleasant.

God is **patient.** He doesn't fly off the handle when we make mistakes.

1. How has your knowledge of who God is and how He works affected your worship of Him?

____

____

____

2. How can your knowledge of who God is and how He works shape how you collectively treat your players and your team?

____

____

____

____

▸WORSHIP THE LORD GRATEFULLY

Luke 17:11-19

[11] On the way to Jerusalem he was passing along between Samaria and Galilee. [12] And as
he entered a village, he was met by ten lepers, who stood at a distance [13] and lifted up their
voices, saying, "Jesus, Master, have mercy on us." [14] When he saw them he said to them, "Go
and show yourselves to the priests." And as they went they were cleansed. [15] Then one of them,
when he saw that he was healed, turned back, praising God with a loud voice; [16] and he fell
on his face at Jesus' feet, giving him thanks. Now he was a Samaritan. [17] Then Jesus answered,
"Were not ten cleansed? Where are the nine? [18] Was no one found to return and give praise
to God except this foreigner?" [19] And he said to him, "Rise and go your way; your faith has
made you well."

For a moment, put yourself in the sandals of one of the lepers. Your family members, friends, and community all have shunned you. On top of your social ostracization, you are physically miserable and utterly void of hope.

Then, when you see Jesus entering your village, you and your fellow lepers beg Him to cleanse you. He instructs all of you to present yourselves to the priests. You have no idea how that will help, but with nothing to lose, you and your fellow lepers start on your way to the priests.

On your trek, you realize your leprosy has vanished and your entire body has been cleansed. The leprosy is gone! And, with it, all your misery!

You know that Jesus was responsible, so how do you feel? How do you respond?

With jump-up-down happiness and immense gratitude, right?

Well, let's bring Jesus' cleansing of the 10 lepers home today. In doing so, we will think of leprosy as representing our sin contamination.

However, your sickness and misery were far worse than physical leprosy. You were eternally dead in your trespasses and sins. You were destined for eternal judgment. But God made you alive in Jesus and gave you an eternal home in His kingdom.

1. In the Psalm, we are to enter His gates with thanksgiving and His courts with praise (verse 4). How might you want these words to describe you as you get ready for each practice and competition?

____

____

____

____

____

2. How might being grateful to God for what He has done in your life affect how you strategize for each competition?

____

____

____

____

____

GAME CHANGER

> *"It is he who made us, and we are his;*
> *we are his people, and the sheep of his pasture."*

The Bible often uses the illustration of a shepherd and his sheep to paint the picture of God's protective relationship with His people. Because God protects and provides for His sheep, the Children of Israel, they could worship Him with confidence that their Shepherd would never leave their side.

Isn't that also the confidence we can have because of Jesus' promise:

> *"I am the good shepherd. The good shepherd lays down his life for his sheep." - John 10:11*

Jesus is the ultimate Game-Changer. First, He laid down His life to save His sheep from being devoured by eternal death. Then, He picked His life back up, giving His sheep the ABUNDANT LIFE.

Just as the psalmist did, we can praise God because we are Christ's sheep, and He is our Good Shepherd.

ONE BIG THING

What is the most significant lesson for you from this chapter?

____

____

____

____

____

____

____

IMPACT PRAYER

Father in Heaven, You are worthy of all praise, honor, and glory. You are good, faithful, and true. You have rescued us from our sins and brought us back into your fold. Help us live enthusiastically for your praise and be ready to publicly honor Your Name through adoration, song, thanksgiving, and prayer. Before we are coaches, we are worshipers. Help us coach from a place of passionate worship. For the glory of Jesus, Amen.

KINGDOM COACHING

Commit to each coaching situation as a praise to God for who He is and what He has done for you.

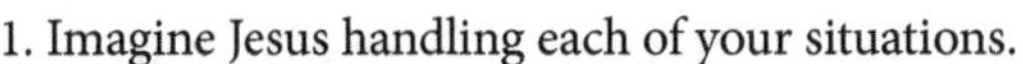

1. Imagine Jesus handling each of your situations.

   Developing weekly practice plan.

   Each conversation.

   Each instruction.

   Correcting.

   Disciplining.

2. As your praise of God, allow Jesus to do through you what He would do. It's your "singing" to God…and in perfect tune.

NOTES:

★ ★ ★

CHAPTER EIGHT

WORSHIPFUL COACHES GIVE GOD THANKS

PSALM 107

STUDY STARTER

On Christmas morning of 2015, a dad videoed his four-year-old child opening a neatly packaged gift. The child enthusiastically tore into the gift. As the little boy's eyes fixed on a huge, dark green avocado, his response was not disdain, confusion, or discouragement. Instead, he immediately replied, "It's an avocado!!! Thaaaaaanks!!!"

Then he put the avocado aside and reached for the next gift. By the way, you can see the video on YouTube under "Boy Gets Avocado for Christmas.

As worshipers of God, sadly, we can treat the profound goodness and extravagant love of almighty God like it is no more than an avocado. "It's the grace of God! Thaaaaaanks."...Then, onto the next gift.

In Psalm 107, the psalmist will help us have a deeper reverence for the goodness of God and a more consistent gratitude for His love. So, let's dive in with a desire to become thankful worshipers of God.

STUDY PASSAGE

107 [1]*Oh give **thanks** to the Lord, for he is good,*
for his steadfast love endures forever!
[2] *Let the redeemed of the Lord say so,*
whom he has redeemed from trouble
[3] *and gathered in from the lands,*
from the east and from the west,
from the north and from the south.
[4] *Some wandered in desert wastes,*
finding no way to a city to dwell in;
[5] *hungry and thirsty,*
their soul fainted within them.

6 *Then they cried to the Lord in their trouble,*
and he delivered them from their distress.
7 *He led them by a straight way*
till they reached a city to dwell in.
8 *Let them* **thank** *the Lord for his steadfast love,*
for his wondrous works to the children of man!
9 *For he satisfies the longing soul,*
and the hungry soul he fills with good things.

10 *Some sat in darkness and in the shadow of death,*
prisoners in affliction and in irons,
11 *for they had rebelled against the words of God,*
and spurned the counsel of the Most High.
12 *So he bowed their hearts down with hard labor;*
they fell down, with none to help.
13 *Then they cried to the Lord in their trouble,*
and he delivered them from their distress.
14 *He brought them out of darkness and the shadow of death,*
and burst their bonds apart.
15 *Let them* **thank** *the Lord for his steadfast love,*
for his wondrous works to the children of man!

16 *For he shatters the doors of bronze*
and cuts in two the bars of iron.
17 *Some were fools through their sinful ways,*
and because of their iniquities suffered affliction;
18 *they loathed any kind of food,*
and they drew near to the gates of death.
19 *Then they cried to the Lord in their trouble,*
and he delivered them from their distress.
20 *He sent out his word and healed them,*
and delivered them from their destruction.
21 *Let them* **thank** *the Lord for his steadfast love,*

for his wondrous works to the children of man!
22 *And let them offer sacrifices of* ***thanksgiving****,*
and tell of his deeds in ***songs of joy****!*

23 *Some went down to the sea in ships,*
doing business on the great waters;
24 *they saw the deeds of the Lord,*
his wondrous works in the deep.
25 *For he commanded and raised the stormy wind,*
which lifted up the waves of the sea.
26 *They mounted up to heaven; they went down to the depths;*
their courage melted away in their evil plight;
27 *they reeled and staggered like drunken men*
and were at their wits' end.
28 *Then they cried to the Lord in their trouble,*
and he delivered them from their distress.
29 *He made the storm be still,*
and the waves of the sea were hushed.
30 *Then they were glad that the waters were quiet,*
and he brought them to their desired haven.
31 *Let them* ***thank*** *the Lord for his steadfast love,*
for his wondrous works to the children of man!
32 *Let them* ***extol*** *him in the congregation of the people,*
and ***praise*** *him in the assembly of the elders.*

33 *He turns rivers into a desert,*
springs of water into thirsty ground,
34 *a fruitful land into a salty waste,*
because of the evil of its inhabitants.
35 *He turns a desert into pools of water,*
a parched land into springs of water.
36 *And there he lets the hungry dwell,*
and they establish a city to live in;

37 *they sow fields and plant vineyards*
and get a fruitful yield.
38 *By his blessing they multiply greatly,*
and he does not let their livestock diminish.
39 *When they are diminished and brought low*
through oppression, evil, and sorrow,
40 *he pours contempt on princes*
and makes them wander in trackless wastes;
41 *but he raises up the needy out of affliction*
and makes their families like flocks.
42 *The upright see it and are glad,*
and all wickedness shuts its mouth.
43 *Whoever is wise, let him attend to these things;*
let them ***consider*** *the steadfast love of the Lord.*

STUDY HELP

- ***"From the east and from the west, from the north and from the south"*** – The redemption of God is exclusive and inclusive. Only those who hope in God will be redeemed, but this hope is offered to all people from east to west and north to south.

- ***"In irons"*** – God doesn't simply redeem people from different locations, he redeems people from the most radical of circumstances. Even the prisoner has been freed from his chains.

- ***"Extol"*** – To extol means to exalt. So, the role of the redeemed is to exalt the character and work of God to those around him.

STUDY QUESTIONS

1. Psalm 107 is an exposition of God's goodness. List five ways the psalm describes His goodness.

____

____

____

____

____

2. God's people have found themselves in difficult circumstances. They've "cried out" to Him for help. How has He responded to their cries (vv. 6-7, 13, 19, 30, etc.)?

____

____

____

3. The final verse in this psalm instructs the worshiper to "consider" the steadfast love of the Lord. That word means "to discern, scrutinize, understand". Look at verses 33-43 again and "consider" God's righteous love for His people, list four of the eight action verbs the psalmist used to describe God's righteous love.

____

____

____

____

4. God is not only good, but He is also powerful. Of course, without His power, His goodness is meaningless. List three ways Psalm 107 describes the unmatched power of God.

5. How many times does the psalmist instruct worshipers to have expressions of gratitude to God? Consider the bolded words.

6. God's goodness and steadfast love require a proper response. A worshipful coach does not merely agree that God is good; they respond to that goodness with thanksgiving and praise. If you were to look for God's goodness in your practices, how might you express your thankfulness when you see it?

7. Followers of Jesus Christ should be the most thankful people in the world. Do you agree with this statement? Why or why not?

8. How might your attitude of thankfulness affect how you approach each practice?

STUDY SUMMARY

The response of a worshiper who considers God's goodness and steadfast love for His people is adoration and thanksgiving.

COACHING CONNECTION

A worshipful coach continually considers the goodness of God, continually expresses their thankfulness to God, and continually puts a spotlight on God's greatness in their athletic arena.

KEYS TO WINNING

▸ **VIDEO GUIDE AT KINGDOMSPORTS.ONLINE**

▸ CONSIDER GOD

Consider His Goodness:

- **God is good in His nature.** Goodness is what God is. God's love is good. God's righteousness is good. God's holiness is good. God's judgments are good. God's wrath is good. God's will is good. Everything about God is good.
- **God is the source of all goodness.** It is not possible to have goodness without God. And it is not possible to have God without goodness. So, if you've ever experienced anything good, it came from God because you can't have true goodness without Him. With that in mind, what might you conclude if you can't see something good

in a practice or competition?

- **God is always good.** There has never been a moment in which God was not good. God is not like Dr. Jekyll and Mr. Hyde. He's not good in one moment and bad in another. So, since He is always good, what might you be learning about your fellowship with God if your feelings toward an athlete depend on how well they are doing.
- **God is good in His works.** Everything that God does is good. We have difficulty understanding that sometimes, but it is nevertheless true.

How has God been good to you?

1. Physically?

____

____

____

2. Materially?

____

____

____

3. Circumstantially?

____

____

____

4. Relationally?

____

____

____

5. Spiritually?

____

____

Consider His Steadfast Love:

- **His love is Unrestrained** – God doesn't hold portions of His love back from us to see how we're going to respond. He's not like people who restrain themselves from complete love until they gauge the other person's commitment level. No, God is all in! He doesn't hold anything back.

- **His love is Relentless** – God pursues you with His love. He is not passive. He doesn't say, "Well, if you want some of my love, you're going to have to come and get it." No, He tracks us down so that He can deposit His love on us.

- **His love is Faithful** – God's love never fails. Everything else fails at some point: people, technology, buildings, teams, everything. But God's love never fails. His love is faithful.

- **His love is Passionate** – There is nothing vanilla about God's love. His love is passionate. Consider these passages: **John 3:16** – *"For God so loved the world, that he gave his only Son, that whoever believes in him should not perish but have eternal life.* **Eph 2:4-6** – *But God, being rich in mercy, because of the great love with which he loved us, even when we were dead in our trespasses, made us alive together with Christ—by grace you have been saved—and raised us up with him and seated us with him in the heavenly places in Christ Jesus.*

Describe a time when you experienced God's extravagant, passionate, personal love.

▸ CRY OUT TO GOD

Unless you are uniquely disciplined to cry out to God, you likely suffer from a dispassionate communication line with your Deliverer. In other words, the less vibrant your prayer life is, the less you see your desperate or urgent need for God.

The fact is you are desperate for God. And without a flood of His goodness and steadfast love into your life, you are destined for despair.

Many of God's faithful followers knew this very well. King David was desperate for forgiveness and cried out to God for reconciliation. Saul of Tarsus was desperate to know the identity behind the blinding light, and he cried out, "Who are you, Lord?" The thief on the cross was desperate for salvation and cried, "Remember me when You enter your kingdom." Finally, Jairus was desperate for his daughter's healing and cried out for Jesus to heal her.

Worshipful coaches are marked by crying out to God for themselves, their families, friends, colleagues, and players. What steps can you take to cultivate a lifestyle of "crying out" to God for yourself and others?

____

____

____

▸ CELEBRATE GOD

The essence of worship is celebration. True worship is the celebration of being in a covenant relationship with the God of Heaven and Earth. Worship involves confession, praise, thanksgiving, trust, obedience, service, and more.

But at its very core, worship is celebrating the fact that you are in communion with God Himself. Therefore, just as followers of Christ should be the most thankful people on earth, they should also be the most enthusiastic.

If Jesus is your Savior, you have been redeemed, adopted, justified, forgiven, Spirit-filled, and empowered for a life full of eternal purpose. There is nothing more worthy to celebrate regularly than this.

A non-celebratory Christian is a contradiction of terms and an affront to the goodness of God. List ways that you can consistently celebrate God's goodness and steadfast love:

1. Personally?

____

____

2. With Your Family?

3. With Your Church?

4. With Your Friends?

5. With Your Christian Players?

GAME CHANGER

> ***"Then they cried to the Lord in their trouble,***
> ***and he delivered them from their distress."***

This psalm repetitiously demonstrates God's deliverance of His people from their distress. They were thirsty; He gave them water. They were hungry; He gave them food. They were oppressed; He rescued them. They were discouraged; He lifted them up.

Life is full of distress. The most evident distress is often the ones we physically or emotionally feel pain, hunger, thirst, sickness, heartbreak, and failure. But the distress that is most perilous is that of sin.

Remember Psalm 51. David said he was conceived in sin. How is that? People come out of the womb and into the world as sinners. There's no need to teach a child to lie to save his skin. There's no need to teach a child to be selfish and hoard toys.

All people are inherently sinful. Paul says in Romans 3 that all have sinned and continuously walk in sin. This sin, committed against Holy God, has earned all people eternal punishment. But just as the Lord delivered His people from their physical distresses, He also delivers His people from the distress of sin.

Jesus delivers us from the distress of abiding sin by taking out our heart of stone and replacing it with a heart of flesh that beats for His glory. Jesus delivers us from the distress of active sin by giving us His Holy Spirit to guide us through life. And Jesus delivers us from the distress of punishable sin by taking upon Himself the punishment of Hell and providing us the glory of Heaven.

Let us give thanks to the Lord Jesus, our Ultimate Deliverer.

ONE BIG THING

What is the most significant lesson for you from this chapter?

IMPACT PRAYER

Father in Heaven, You are infinitely good. Your steadfast love is immeasurable. Please tether our hearts to your goodness. Help us cry out to You in our desperation and celebrate You in our deliverances. Use the authenticity of our worship to draw others to Jesus, our ultimate Deliverer. Amen.

KINGDOM COACHING

Look for three expressions of God's goodness in each practice and competition and thank Him each time you see one.

Interestingly, a lifestyle of thanks gives us physical and emotional benefits. Dr. Robert Emmons, a professor of psychology at the University of California at Davis, regarded as one of the world's leading scientific experts on the power of gratitude—or living a life of thankfulness—lists a few of those benefits.

Among them are a stronger immune system, fewer aches and pains, lower blood pressure, more restful sleep, more joy and pleasure, and more positive emotions.

So, as a worshipful coach with your commitment to thank God for His expressions of goodness in your practices and competitions, you'll be physically and emotionally healthier as a result.

★ ★ ★

CHAPTER NINE

WORSHIPFUL COACHES PERSONALIZE THEOLOGY

PSALM 139

STUDY STARTER

James and Timmy, two young brothers, were always getting into trouble doing mischievous things. Then, one day, their school's principal phoned their mom: "You're going to have to come get your boys. They've done it again!"

The frazzled mother didn't know what to do with them. So, she took them down to the community church to meet with the pastor. He agreed to counsel them, looking forward to trying a new approach he had just learned.

He sat Timmy down outside his office while he talked with James inside his office. This is how it went.

Pastor: "James, where is God?"

James looked confused and didn't answer.

Pastor: "James, where is God?"

James, still confused, looked up and down and from side to side, but still no answer.

Pastor: "Son, now speak to me. Where is God?"

James jumps up, rushes out the door, grabs Timmy, and the two run three miles without stopping to their secret hiding place in the woods. Then, slumped over and out of breath, James looks Timmy in the eyes and frantically says, "Timmy, God's missing! And the pastor thinks we had something to do with it!"

Now, that's a funny story. But sadly, even though James and Timmy have nothing to do with it, God is missing in the hearts and minds of many Christians today. As believers, we can still have wrong or incomplete thoughts about God.

Sometimes we use our logic and personal feelings instead of the Scriptures to draw conclusions about God. For example, we might even wrongly conclude that God is too busy for us, too removed, or maybe too disappointed in us to make time for us.

Have you ever considered how small your life is in the big scheme? Perhaps you have asked questions like, "How much time does God really spend thinking about me, my life, my family, my team, and my schedule?"

Sure, you know that God loves you and promises to take care of you. But how personal can you expect the God of the universe to be with you? After all, He is the Sovereign Creator of everything.

He governs Heaven. He rules over angels. He sustains all the galaxies. He reigns over the solar systems and keeps them in their proper places. He holds the earth on its proper axis, rotating it around the sun, keeping it 94,000,000 miles away from it so that we don't burn up or freeze. I mean, just how personal is that kind of God going to be with you?

I have good news. According to Psalm 139, God is both infinite and intimate. He is both powerful and personal. Thus, He is intimately involved in your life. There is nothing in your life that God is unconcerned about. There is nothing in your life that God is unaware of. Even now, He is paying close attention to you while you are reading this sentence.

Let's look at Psalm 139 to get a tighter grip on God, who is infinite and intimate.

STUDY PASSAGE

139 TO THE CHOIRMASTER: A PSALM OF DAVID

[1] *O Lord, you have searched me and known me!*

[2] *You know when I sit down and when I rise up;*
you discern my thoughts from afar.

[3] *You search out my path and my lying down*
and are acquainted with all my ways.

[4] *Even before a word is on my tongue,*
behold, O Lord, you know it altogether.

[5] *You hem me in, behind and before,*
and lay your hand upon me.

[6] *Such knowledge is too wonderful for me;*

it is high; I cannot attain it.

7 *Where shall I go from your Spirit?*

Or where shall I flee from your presence?

8 *If I ascend to heaven, you are there!*

If I make my bed in Sheol, you are there!

9 *If I take the wings of the morning*

and dwell in the uttermost parts of the sea,

10 *even there your hand shall lead me,*

and your right hand shall hold me.

11 *If I say, "Surely the darkness shall cover me,*

and the light about me be night,"

12 *even the darkness is not dark to you;*

the night is bright as the day,

for darkness is as light with you.

13 *For you formed my inward parts;*

you knitted me together in my mother's womb.

14 *I praise you, for I am fearfully and wonderfully made.*

Wonderful are your works;

my soul knows it very well.

15 *My frame was not hidden from you,*

when I was being made in secret,

intricately woven in the depths of the earth.

16 *Your eyes saw my unformed substance;*

in your book were written, every one of them,

the days that were formed for me,

when as yet there was none of them.

17 *How precious to me are your thoughts, O God!*

How vast is the sum of them!

18 *If I would count them, they are more than the sand.*

I awake, and I am still with you.

[19] *Oh that you would slay the wicked, O God!*

O men of blood, depart from me!

[20] *They speak against you with malicious intent;*

your enemies take your name in vain.

[21] *Do I not hate those who hate you, O Lord?*

And do I not loathe those who rise up against you?

[22] *I hate them with complete hatred;*

I count them my enemies.

[23] *Search me, O God, and know my heart!*

Try me and know my thoughts!

[24] *And see if there be any grievous way in me,*

and lead me in the way everlasting!

STUDY HELP

- ***"searched"*** - to investigate, search out, discover, test, and examine. It is translated in other places as "dig." The idea here is that God makes a full investigation of a person's life. He searches and sifts. As a master detective, God leaves no stone unturned. He exercises perfect scrutiny.
- ***"known"*** - Not only does God search a person, knowing all the details about the person, but He also ***"knows"*** that person.
- ***"You hem me in"*** - Just as a parent protectively hovers over a baby trying to take her first steps; God hems in His children to protect them along life's journey.
- ***"Sheol"*** - the place of the dead.
- ***"intricately woven"*** - This term was used for embroidery, the intricate design of materials. The picture is one of a weaver or knitter who weaves and embroiders complex patterns and colors together to form a beautiful design. The psalmist's point is that *God does not wait and see what He can do with the hand He is dealt.* No! He forms and fashions each person specifically, uniquely, and personally for His glory.
- ***"in the depths of the earth"*** - this is a euphemism for the womb of the mother.

- ***"more than the sand"*** - If you Google "how many grains of sand are on the earth?" the first answer you will receive is: 7.5 sextillion. That's 7,500,000,000,000,000,000. The psalmist asserts that God's thoughts toward him are more than the sand. That's a pretty personal God!
- ***"the wicked"*** - those who hate God and God's people. They speak against God and take His name in vain (Exodus 20:7). They reject His love, rebel against His authority, ignore His holiness, and thumb their nose at His glory. They consider the glorious truth of God's omniscience, omnipresence, and omnipotence over their lives to be irrelevant.
- ***"hate"*** – David felt a strong allegiance to God. He knew that a person who loves God also hates sin. God hates sin and is committed to punishing it. That's what the cross is all about. David's graphic and repetitious expressions of hatred are surprising. But David wanted to be clear about where he stood with those who hated God.

STUDY QUESTIONS

1. We can more fully grasp the personal nature of God's connection to the psalmist by counting the number of times the psalmist uses the designations **Lord** and **God** and the second-person personal pronouns **you** and **your.** How many times for each?

Lord and God =

You and your =

2. Again, to more fully grasp the personal nature of God's connection to the psalmist, how often did he use the first-person personal pronouns **I, me,** and **my?** ___

3. In verses 1-6, what is the psalmist's response to the supernatural, complete knowledge that God possesses of his life, words, and ways?

___

___

___

4. How does knowing that God has complete knowledge of you and all the details of your team and season affect your approach to each practice and competition?

___

___

___

5. From verses 7-12, how would you describe the presence of God?

___

___

___

6. From verses 13-18, what is the psalmist's response to God's creative power and detailed design of his body and life?

___

___

___

7. From verses 19-24, how would you describe David's posture towards God's enemies, and why was he postured that way?

___

___

___

8. How can David's posture and a posture of loving compassion work together?

___

___

___

9. From verses 23-24, what four requests does he make of God and why does he make them?

___

___

___

___

STUDY SUMMARY

God is both infinite *and* intimate. He is both powerful *and* personal. Therefore, He can be trusted. Therefore, worshipers have every reason to confidently give Him their whole hearts.

COACHING CONNECTION

As a worshipful coach, in each practice and competition, you can celebrate God's knowledge of you, His presence with you, His love for you, and His transforming power in you.

KEYS TO WINNING

▶ **VIDEO GUIDE AT KINGDOMSPORTS.ONLINE**

Theology is the study of God, His character, attributes, ways, works, and will. Therefore, theology is a good and necessary discipline for every worshiper, including worshipful coaches.

Theology is only profitable once it becomes *personal*. You must take what you know about God and apply those truths to your own life. That is precisely what the psalmist models for us in Psalm 139. He personalizes the truths he knows about God.

If you're going to succeed as a worshipful coach, you must know these four truths:

▸ GOD KNOWS YOU (vv. 1-6)

This section personalizes the doctrine of God's Omniscience, which says that God possesses perfect knowledge. He knows everything about everything, and He has never learned anything.

God knows who you are. He ***"searches"*** you. Hebrews 4:13 tells us that "there is no creature hidden from God's sight, but all things are naked and open to the eyes of Him to whom we must give account." Even now, God is searching you out, digging through the rubble of your heart, and investigating your thoughts, motives, and desires.

Not only does God search you, but He also ***"knows"*** you. God is not like a frustrated private investigator who unsuccessfully searches and searches for information that he cannot find. No, God always finds what He is looking for. He knows all the details and all the issues. He has a full and intimate knowledge of who you are, what you do, where you go, what you say, how you think, and what you want. He "understands" you from front to back and from top to bottom.

More than that, God knows what you need. David says, *"You hem me in, behind and before."* He means, "You enclose me, You hedge me in, You surround me." God protects us just as a mother surrounds—hovers over, and protects—her baby daughter trying to walk.

This truth is mind-boggling. Notice that David says that it is *"too wonderful for"* him. Divine omniscience is too high for us humans to comprehend. It is so incomprehensible that we can only be in awe of it. At this marvelous truth, we can echo the words of Romans 11:33, *"O the depths of the wisdom and knowledge of God. How unsearchable His thoughts and unfathomable His ways!"*

How should God's omniscience shape how you think, live, and lead daily?

Think:

____

____

____

Live:

Lead:

▸ GOD HOLDS YOU (vv. 7-12)

This section personalizes the doctrine of God's Omnipresence, which says that God is present at every point of space in the totality of His being. Shedd's Theology says it this way, "The whole essence of God is here, there, and everywhere."

You cannot escape God's presence. If you go to Heaven, He is there. If you go to Hell, He is there. If you go out to sea, He is there. As you may recall, Jonah tried the whole "heading out to sea" thing to escape the presence of God. It didn't work for him! And it won't work for us either.

In Jeremiah 23:24, God says, "*Can anyone hide himself in secret places, so I shall not see him?" says the LORD; "Do I not fill heaven and earth?"* says the LORD. God is everywhere. He is always in all places with all of His being.

More than that, God is everywhere *with* you! Wherever you go, God is there. Wherever you stay, God is there. Wherever you sleep, God is there. Wherever you play, God is there. Wherever you plan, God is there. Wherever you practice, God is there. Wherever you compete, God is there.

William Blake wrote, "Do not think you can sigh a sigh and your Maker is not by; Do not think you can weep a tear and your Maker is not near."

And, of course, David wrote these comforting words in Psalm 23:1-4: "The LORD is my shepherd; I shall not want. He makes me to lie down in green pastures; He leads me beside the still waters. He restores my soul; He leads me in the paths of righteousness For His name's sake. Yea, though I walk through the valley of the shadow of death, I will fear no evil; *For You are with me*; Your rod and Your staff, they comfort me."

Just as God was with David, He is with you. He is with you at home, work, practice, and competitions. He is with you when you drive, walk, run, and workout. He is with you when you plan, scheme, and watch film. He is with you when you eat, sleep, and rest. He is with you when you win, lose, and get rained out. He is with you when you succeed and fail. He is with you when you thrive and suffer. He is always with you, and He never leaves you.

Consider the powerful poem, *Footprints in the Sand*, by Mary Stevenson.

One night I dreamed a dream. I was walking along the beach with my Lord. Across the dark sky flashed scenes from my life. For each scene, I noticed two sets of footprints in the sand, one belonging to me and one to my Lord.

When the last scene of my life shot before me I looked back at the footprints in the sand. There was only one set of footprints. I realized that this was at the lowest and saddest times of my life. This always bothered me and I questioned the Lord about my dilemma.

"Lord, You told me when I decided to follow You, You would walk and talk with me all the way. But I'm aware that during the most troublesome times of my life there is only one set of footprints. I just don't understand why, when I need You most, You leave me."

He whispered, "My precious child, I love you and will never leave you, never, ever, during your trials and testings. When you saw only one set of footprints, it was then that I carried you."

God holds you in your most challenging days. You are not alone. You are not abandoned. You are not without help. He is with you and for you. So how should God's omnipresence shape how you think, live, and lead each day?

Think:

____

____

____

Live:

___

___

___

Lead:

___

___

___

▸ GOD LOVES YOU (vv. 13-18)

This section personalizes the doctrine of God's Omnipotence, which says that God is all-powerful. He made everything, sustains everything, and rules over everything. Not only is He all-powerful in a massive way, but He is also all-powerful in a very intimate, personal way.

God made you. He intricately formed your body. He sovereignly watched over your development while in your mother's womb. You are no accident. You are not a product of coincidence.

In Jeremiah 1:5, the Lord informs his prophet about the beginning stages of his life, *"Before I formed you in the womb I knew you; Before you were born I sanctified you; I ordained you a prophet to the nations."* God conceived of you in eternity past and then followed through when He formed you in your mother's womb.

For this reason, God is praiseworthy. He fearfully and wonderfully made you. Like David, you should be astounded at the magnificence of God's creative ability.

The human body is one of the most complex and beautifully designed systems in the entire universe. Your body is a testament to the complexity and beauty of the Lord's divine design.

Every single day your heart beats over 100,000 times. Your blood travels over 12,000 miles. You breathe 23,000 times. You inhale over 2000 gallons of air. You move 750 muscles. You exercise 7,000,000 brain cells. Every single day.

That's remarkable! The Divine Creator has woven you in such an intricate way that the functions of your body are simply unfathomable.

Consider the man born blind in John 9:1-3: *Now as Jesus passed by, He saw a man who was blind from birth. And His disciples asked Him, saying, "Rabbi, who sinned, this man or his parents, that he was born blind?"* Jesus answered, *"Neither this man nor his parents sinned, but that the works of God should be revealed in him."*

Jesus goes on to bring sight to the blind man. But embedded in the man's life story is the same message that is embedded in your life story: God has made you the way you are to work His works in and through you.

God loves you immeasurably. In your own body, there is an unimaginable wealth of detail and design, and every one of those details comes from the thoughts of God. This proves the infinite commitment God has toward you as a person. He not only knows the number of hairs on your head, but He patterned the hairs on your head for His glory. Your hair or lack of it is part of God's design.

Like most people, you might be self-conscious about some physical features you have… your height, weight, facial features, muscle mass, hair color, athleticism, etc. As a result, you may be tempted to think, *If God is so powerful and particular in creating me, why did He make me with such deficiencies?*

God made you the way you are so He can uniquely glorify Himself through your height, strength, physical features, handicap, or whatever. God's design is to glorify Himself through the unique expression of who you are.

So, stop using your self-diagnosed deficiencies as occasions for complaint or self-pity. Instead, start thanking God for how he has uniquely made you. Use your uniqueness for His glory. You are not a product of some coincidence. You are not a result of chance. God specially and precisely created you for His glory.

How should God's omnipotence shape how you think, live, and lead others daily?

Think:

Live:

Lead:

▸ GOD CHANGES YOU (vv. 19-24)

Psalm 139 has already taught the doctrines of God's Omniscience, Omnipresence, and Omnipotence. In this section, we see the doctrine of God's Holiness played out in a personal way.

God's Holiness can be described as sinlessness, separateness, and supremacy. He is without sin. He is unlike us. He is higher than us. Richard Lints says, "The holiness of God refers to His absolute moral purity and absolute moral distance between Him and us."

David desired to respond to God's infinite greatness in a way that honored Him. He wanted nothing to do with evil men. David knew the same time-tested relationship principles we know:

- Bad company corrupt good morals.
- Birds of a feather flock together.
- Water always seeks its own level.
- If you want to know who you are, look at your five closest friends.

David separated himself from those who hated God and prayed for God to exercise His justice and judgment on them. He didn't want to be numbered with those rebelling against the omniscient, omnipresent, and omnipotent God.

But he also knew that he was sinful and had the capacity to turn away from the Lord at any time. So, he asked God to search him, to know him, to try him, and to evaluate him so that he could live honorably before the Lord.

David offered himself to God by saying, "Have Your way with me, God. I want to live in communion with You, reflect Your glory, and walk in holiness. I want to fulfill Your calling on my life."

So, David prayed, *"search me…try me…lead me"*. We pray for God's leadership often but rarely plead for Him to search and test our hearts. That seems a bit intrusive! Certainly uncomfortable. If God were to search us and try us, it would leave us in a vulnerable position. But this is the only way for God to truly change us.

> *23 Search me, O God, and know my heart!*
> *Try me and know my thoughts!*
> *24 And see if there be any grievous way in me,*
> *and lead me in the way everlasting!*

Are you willing to make that your prayer? Are you willing for God to uncover fear, anxiety, pride, or idolatry? Such a prayer might invite pain. But there is no need to be afraid. God loves you, and He will be with you through it all. He wants what is the very best for you.

The only way for that to happen is to open yourself up to the all-knowing, all-present, all-powerful God. J.I. Packer said it well: "*I am graven on the palms of His hands. I am never out of his mind. I know Him because He first knew me. He knows me as a friend. There is no moment when His eye is off me or His attention distracted from me…. God is taking knowledge of me in love and watching over me for my good.*"

How should God's holiness shape how you think, live, and lead others daily?

Think:

Live:

Lead:

GAME CHANGER

> *"Where shall I go from your Spirit?*
> *Or where shall I flee from your presence?*
> *If I ascend to heaven, you are there!*
> *If I make my bed in Sheol, you are there..."*

As David wrote this Psalm, God's presence was continual, powerful, and spiritual. He was always present with His people, but not necessarily in a physical way. God led, protected, guided, and comforted his people. But they could not *see* Him, *touch* Him, or *walk* next to Him...until Jesus came.

Jesus is Immanuel – *"God with us."* Jesus is fully God and fully man. He took on human flesh to dwell with us and walk the earth as a human. But He did something no human has ever done – He lived perfectly and sinlessly. He earned what we couldn't, eternal life with God.

After receiving the due penalty for our sins, He rose from the dead, ascended into heaven, and sent His Spirit to live inside every person who believes in Him. The Spirit of Jesus now dwells in the heart of every person who follows Him (Romans 8:9).

So not only can we be assured that the omnipresent God is with us, but we can also have confidence that He is in us. And not only is He in us, but He is guiding us. And not only is He guiding us, but He is protecting us in our union with Him until that final day when Jesus makes all things new.

Jesus is the ultimate Game Changer. Through Him, we can enjoy God's very presence and power every day.

ONE BIG THING

What is the most significant lesson for you to take with you from this chapter?

____

____

____

____

____

____

____

____

IMPACT PRAYER

Father in Heaven, You are worthy of all praise and honor. You are the all-knowing, all-present, all-powerful, and all-holy God. There is nothing you don't know, nothing you don't see, nothing you can't do. You do what You want, when You want, with whom You want. Thank You for rescuing us from our sins and giving us a heart to worship You forever. Please help us think, live, and lead in a way that puts a spotlight on Your infinite worth. For the glory of Jesus, Amen.

KINGDOM COACHING

Be aware of God's presence in each detail of your practices and competitions as you carry out your Playbook for Coaching Jesus' Way.

With this awareness, even "routine" drills are no longer routine. At any nanosecond, God will either do or allow whatever He wants in His larger scheme of things. He is totally involved.

As you are aware of God's presence, you can have intimate fellowship with Him, even in the wildest of practices and competitions.

NOTES:

★ ★ ★

CHAPTER TEN

WORSHIPFUL COACHES PRAISE THE LORD

PSALM 150

STUDY STARTER

More than anything else, you were created to worship God. Consider these statements from some renowned theologians down through the ages.

- "We should not be concerned about working for God until we have learned the meaning and the delight of worshiping Him." - A.W. Tozer
- "Christian worship is the most momentous, the most urgent, the most glorious action that can take place in human life." - Karl Barth
- "Man is never more truly man than when he worships God" - James B. Torrance
- "God has given us the gift of sports so that we might enjoy them for His glory. Our athletic abilities were given to us by God so that we might use them for His glory. Let's not receive these gifts passively! Millions of people enjoy the gift of sports without ever uttering a word of thanks or praise to the glorious Giver of gifts. As Christians we know the author of every good and perfect gift. Let us resolve that whenever we're enjoying sports, whether playing or watching them, we will thank our extravagantly lavish God who gives us such wonderful gifts." – Stephen Altrogge

Wow! According to these theologians, worship is the most significant thing you can do with your life. It definitely was for the apostle Paul.

In Romans 12:1, he doubled down on worship's necessity and holistic nature when he wrote: "Present your bodies as a living sacrifice, holy and acceptable to God, which is your spiritual worship."

When everything is stripped down to its very core, the heart, and soul of worship are to give praise to God. In your coaching, give praise to God. In your teaching, give praise to God. In your friendships, give praise to God. In your family, give praise to God. In your church, give praise to God. In everything you do, give praise to God.

But how do we praise Him?

That's what Psalm 150 will be teaching us.

STUDY PASSAGE

150 [1]*Praise the Lord!*

Praise God in his sanctuary;

praise him in his mighty heavens!

[2] *Praise him for his mighty deeds;*

praise him according to his excellent greatness!

[3] *Praise him with trumpet sound;*

praise him with lute and harp!

[4] *Praise him with tambourine and dance;*

praise him with strings and pipe!

[5] *Praise him with sounding cymbals;*

praise him with loud clashing cymbals!

[6] *Let everything that has breath praise the Lord!*

Praise the Lord!

STUDY HELP

- ***"Praise"*** - In this psalm, the Hebrew word for praise is halal. It conveys a natural and enthusiastic response of boasting about someone or something worthy of praise. In the overwhelming number of times in the Old Testament, praise is often rendered to God. The obligation to praise the Lord primarily rested on the people of God.

  Psalm 22:23 says, "*You who fear the LORD, praise Him! All you descendants of Jacob, glorify Him. And fear Him, all you offspring of Israel!*"

  The command to praise the Lord was passed down to every generation. For example, Psalm 78:4 proclaims, "*We will not hide them from their children, telling to the generation to come the praises of the Lord, and His strength and His wonderful works that He has done.*"

  Jeremiah 13:11 tells us that Israel was chosen for God's *praise*. Deuteronomy 26:19 says that Israel was chosen to reflect the Lord's *praiseworthiness* to the world.

So, what kind of praise is being instructed here in Psalm 150? The psalmist instructs worshipers to respond naturally and enthusiastically to boasting in the LORD. He is saying to worshipers, "BOAST IN YOUR GOD! MAKE MUCH OF THE LORD!"

STUDY QUESTIONS

1. What does the many times this psalm calls worshipers to praise the Lord tell us about the importance of praise in the life of the worshiper?

2. God's "sanctuary" is a place set apart for His honor and involves a special recognition of His presence. God's "mighty heavens" refer to the vast expanse of the sky. What do these two terms tell us about where it is fitting to praise God?

3. Which of God's mighty deeds catch your attention the most?

4. List at least three ways the worshipers are called to praise the Lord. In which ways do you praise the Lord most often?

5. What can you do to make praising God more a part of your coaching lifestyle?

6. How might you help others to praise God genuinely?

STUDY SUMMARY

God's great character and mighty works are worthy of abundant praise. Thus, He is worthy of all praise from all people in all places.

COACHING CONNECTION

Worshipful coaches respond with authentic, enthusiastic, and radical praise to God's great character and mighty works. And they long to see others praise God, too.

KEYS TO WINNING

▶ **VIDEO GUIDE AT KINGDOMSPORTS.ONLINE**

▶ THE PLACE OF PRAISE

Praise God in his sanctuary;

Praise him in his mighty heavens

God's sanctuary is His holy place. For the psalmist, that would have been in Jerusalem's temple, the consecrated place of worship for all Israelites.

Yes, worship is a lifestyle (Romans 12:1-2). Yes, our bodies are the temple of the Holy Spirit (1 Corinthians 6:19). The Lord is present with us wherever we go because we are New Covenant worshipers of God and have the Spirit of God living within us.

However, these wonderful realities do not negate the importance of gathering with God's people to worship Him. A sanctuary is wherever God's people gather to worship the Lord. It may be an auditorium with cloth seats. It may be a gymnasium with bleachers. It may be a living room inside a house. It may be an old structure with stained glass windows and wooden pews.

The makeup of a physical structure doesn't make a sanctuary. The people of God do. Wherever God's people are gathered to praise the Lord, there is a sanctuary.

"His mighty heavens" is the heavenly sanctuary of God. It is a place of exquisite beauty and perfection, where light and life proceed from God, undiminished. It is a place where angelic choirs surround the throne of God and sings praises to the Lord because He is who He is, and He does what He does.

1. Describe different places and times you have gathered with God's people in the last 30 days to give Him praise, as well as some of the highlights of those experiences.

A.____

____

B.____

____

C.____

____

D.____

____

2. How can you help your athletes see the hallways, locker room, weight room, and practice field as a place to worship the Lord?

____

____

____

____

▸ THE REASON FOR PRAISE

2 *Praise him for his mighty deeds;*
Praise him according to his excellent greatness.

A God who is not known cannot be worshiped. Allen Ross has said it well, " If worship is ever going to recapture the vision of the holy God of glory, it must begin with the knowledge of the person and works of the LORD."

The psalmist extols us to "praise Him for His mighty deeds". So what are His mighty deeds? One clear way to understand His mighty deeds is through Creation, Providence, Redemption.

In **Creation**, God created everything that we can see, hear, smell, taste, and touch. He created the universe, the earth, the animals, and human beings (His crown jewel). These are some of the most powerful words ever uttered and written, *In the beginning, God created the heavens and the earth* (Genesis 1:1).

God created everything out of nothing (ex nihilo). Just think about that for more than a second. It will blow your mind. One moment there was nothing. Six days later there was everything you and I see, hear, smell, taste, and touch.

In **Providence**, God faithfully guides us along life's journey. Romans 8:28 says, *"We know that in all things God works for the good of those who love Him, who have been called according to His purpose."*

This does not mean that everything that happens to us is good. But it does mean that nothing can ever happen to us apart from God's knowledge, presence, and love. Even in the most desperate circumstances, God always works for our good. That's His providence.

In **Redemption**, God saves His people from the penalty of their sins, eternal death (Romans 6:23). Our God is the God who saves. Just as He rescued Israel from bondage in Egypt, He rescues us from the bondage of our sins. In Jesus Christ, He provides deliverance from the power, pollution, and penalty of sin to the power, purity, and presence of Himself (John 14:6).

Those are His mighty acts and reasons why we praise Him. Now, what are seven mighty acts of the Lord in your life?

1. ______________________________

2. ______________________________

3. ______________________________

4. ______________________________

5. ______________________________

6. ______________________________

7. ______________________________

▸ THE WAY TO PRAISE

[3] *Praise him with trumpet sound;*
praise him with lute and harp!
[4] *Praise him with tambourine and dance;*
praise him with strings and pipe!
[5] *Praise him with sounding cymbals;*
praise him with loud clashing cymbals!

The psalmist describes different types of instruments to use in praising God. Musical instruments can be divided into three basic categories: wind, string, and percussion. The wind instruments include the trumpet and pipe. The string instruments include the lute, harp, and strings. The percussion instruments are the tambourine, sounding cymbals, and loud clashing cymbals.

So, what is the point of using these instruments in worship? God wants our worship of Him to be energetic, enthusiastic, excellent, and awesome. It is the greatest act we can do, so it deserves the greatest collective effort of everyone involved, including musicians. The 16th-century theologian and rebel, Martin Luther, said about musical worship: "Next to the Word of God, the noble art of music is the greatest treasure in the world. It controls our thoughts, minds, hearts, and spirits. A person who does not regard music as a marvelous creation of God does not deserve to be called a human being; he should be permitted to hear nothing but the braying of asses and the grunting of hogs."

Wow! Luther didn't mince words, did he?

Music is one of the most powerful mediums in the world, if not the most powerful. Because God created music for His praise, what are three ways you can praise God through music?

1. ______________________________

____

2. ______________________________

____

3. ______________________________

____

Some of the darkest and most wicked music reverberates from team locker rooms and weight rooms. What steps can you take to protect your athletes from music that distorts their view of God and poisons their character?

____

____

____

▸ THE PEOPLE OF PRAISE

> *6 Let everything that has breath praise the Lord!*
> *Praise the Lord!*

Let everyone who takes a breath give praise to God! For worshipful coaches, embedded in this instruction is an evangelistic call to be on a mission to bring people to God. Consider the vision of global praise in Revelation 5:8-14.

And when he had taken the scroll, the four living creatures and the twenty-four elders fell down before the Lamb, each holding a harp, and golden bowls full of incense, which are the prayers of the saints. And they sang a new song, saying, "Worthy are you to take the scroll and to open its seals, for you were slain, and by your blood you ransomed people for God from every tribe and language and people and nation, and you have made them a kingdom and priests to our God, and they shall reign on the earth."

Then I looked, and I heard around the throne and the living creatures and the elders the voice of many angels, numbering myriads of myriads and thousands of thousands, saying with a loud voice, "Worthy is the Lamb who was slain, to receive power and wealth and wisdom and might and honor and glory and blessing!"

And I heard every creature in heaven and on earth and under the earth and in the sea, and all that is in them, saying, "To him who sits on the throne and to the Lamb be blessing and honor and glory and might forever and ever!"

And the four living creatures said, "Amen!" and the elders fell down and worshiped.

What a vision of universal praise!

As a coach, what lifestyle choices can you establish to help people in your world of influence become worshipers who will gather around the throne and sing, "Worthy is the Lamb who was slain"?

____

____

____

____

GAME CHANGER

> *"Praise him for his* **mighty deeds;**
> *praise him according to his* **excellent greatness!"**

The psalmist recognized that only God is worthy of our highest praise. But even he saw just a shadow of the great work of God that would come.

Today, we think about God's supernatural greatness and His mighty deed in the sacrificial work of Jesus Christ on the cross, leading to His miraculous resurrection. This display of God's love and power fuels in our minds the worship that the psalmist called for in Psalm 150. Consider this glorious truth from Ephesians 1:19-20:

> *(that you may know) what is the immeasurable greatness of his power toward us who believe, according to the working of his great might that he worked in Christ when he raised him from the dead and seated him at his right hand in the heavenly places"*

Jesus is the ultimate game-changer because through His work on the cross and His resurrection from the dead we see and experience the mightiest deeds of God. In Christ's perfect righteousness we see God's excellent greatness. And for that, He is worthy of our eternal praise.

ONE BIG THING

What is the most significant lesson for you to take with you from this chapter?

____

____

____

____

____

____

IMPACT PRAYER

Father in heaven, You have graciously given us the privilege to praise You. Please calibrate our hearts to praise You authentically, enthusiastically, and regularly. Empower us to go out and seek others to do the same. In the name of Jesus, Amen.

KINGDOM COACHING

Release God's Power by Praising Him in Each Situation.

In 1972, author and chaplain, Merlin Carothers, wrote his best-selling book, *Power in Praise.* "We may not understand God's plan or recognize it as good," he wrote, "but when we praise Him for it, we release His power to work in the situation for our good."

Isn't that what you want to happen in your practices and competitions…to witness God's powerful activity in each situation?

As our study draws to a close, why not commit each practice and competition to be an arena in which you, in union with Jesus, will be releasing God's power by praising Him?

When we praise God in a situation, we express our acceptance of the situation and rely on Him to work in it as part of His loving plan for us. Even injuries, insubordinations, slowness in learning, our blowing it, losses…and the list goes on.

As Carothers put it: "I have come to believe that the prayer of praise is the highest form of communion with God, and one that always releases a great deal of power into our lives." That's the power a worshipful coach releases in their sincere praising of God!

CONCLUSION

These are the titles of each chapter you studied. Circle the two that carried the most significance to you in your pursuit of being a worshipful Coach.

Week 1	Psalm 1	Worshipful Coaches DELIGHT IN GOD'S WORD
Week 2	Psalm 2	Worshipful Coaches TRUST IN GOD'S KING
Week 3	Psalm 19	Worshipful Coaches LOVE GOD'S GLORY
Week 4	Psalm 22	Worshipful Coaches REMEMBER THE CROSS
Week 5	Psalm 51	Worshipful Coaches EXPERIENCE RESTORATION
Week 6	Psalm 84	Worshipful Coaches PURSUE GOD'S PRESENCE
Week 7	Psalm 100	Worshipful Coaches GIVE GOD PRAISE
Week 8	Psalm 107	Worshipful Coaches GIVE GOD THANKS
Week 9	Psalm 139	Worshipful Coaches PERSONALIZE THEOLOGY
Week 10	Psalm 150	Worshipful Coaches PRAISE THE LORD

You may want to write a prayer that expresses your desire to be a worshipful coach who praises the Lord and leads others to do the same. You can ask Him to help you grow in the two areas you circled above.

____

____

____

Write down the names and descriptions of the people who participated in this study with you so that you can remember them and the contribution they made to your spiritual growth.

____

____

____

www.ingramcontent.com/pod-product-compliance
Lightning Source LLC
LaVergne TN
LVHW010101110826
845155LV00028B/437

* 9 7 8 1 9 2 9 4 7 8 0 3 3 *